CHRISTOPHER CULPIN
STEVE MASTIN

NAZI GERMANY 1933–45

The authors and publisher wish to thank Victoria Harris for her advice as academic consultant and as a contributor on pages 68–71. All judgements, interpretations and errors remain the responsibility of the authors.

Photo credits

Cover © INTERFOTO/Alamy; **p.3** © Topical Press Agency/Getty Images; **p.7** l © Christopher Culpin, r © Steve Mastin; **p.11** © Bain News Service/Buyenlarge/Getty Images; **p.12** © TopFoto; **p.16** © Bentley Archive/Popperfoto/Getty Images; **p.17** © bpk; **p.19** © Mansell/Time Life Pictures/Getty Images; **p.20** © Universal History Archive/Getty Images; **p.25** © Library of Congress Prints and Photographs Division, LC-DIG-ppmsca-18602; **p.26** © SZ Photo / Scherl; **p.28** © Imagno/Getty Images; **p.34** © SZ Photo / Scherl; **p.36** © The Print Collector / Alamy; **p.39** © 2000 Topham Picturepoint / TopFoto; **p.43** © Everett Collection Historical / Alamy; **p.45** © bpk / Heinrich Hoffmann; **p.47** © Hulton-Deutsch Collection/Corbis; **p.50** © Keystone Pictures USA / Alamy; **p.52** © Deutsches Historisches Museum, Berlin / I. Desnica; **p.55** © INTERFOTO / Alamy; **p.56** © Bundesarchiv Bild 102-04062A, Photo: Georg Pahl; **p.59** © epa european pressphoto agency b.v. / Alamy; **p.61** © Bayerische Staatbibliothek München, Signatur 4 Pol.g. 256 1–6; **p.72** © Lordprice Collection / Alamy; **p.73, 74, 78** © Ivan Vdovin / Alamy; **p.76** © AP/Press Association Images; **p.84** © Walter Ballhause / akg-images; **p.86** © bpk / Kunstbibliothek, SMB / Dietmar Katz; **p.88** © WZ-Bilddienst Bildarchiv; **p.93** © Galerie Bilderwelt/Getty Images; **p.94** © ullsteinbild / TopFoto; **p.97** © Margaret Bourke-White/Time & Life Pictures/Getty Images; **p.98** © Danita Delimont / Alamy; **p.103** © PRISMA ARCHIVO / Alamy; **p.113** © Anthony Potter Collection/Getty Images; **p.116** © Yad Vashem Photo Archive; **p.118** © IMAGNO / Austrian Archives / TopFoto; **p.120** © PRISMA ARCHIVO / Alamy; **p.122** © INTERFOTO / Alamy; **p.125** © akg-images / RIA Nowosti; **p.132** © Staatsarchiv Bremen (Photographer: Walter Cüppers); **p.134** © William Vandivert/Time Life Pictures/Getty Images; **p.139** © Fred Ramage/Keystone/Getty Images.

Text credits

p.3 Alfons Heck: extract from *A Child of Hitler: Germany in the days when God wore a swastika (Renaissance House, 1985)*; **p.9** Hannah Arendt: extract from *The Origins of Totalitarianism (Harcourt, Brace Jovanovich, 1973)*; **p.9** Hans Mommsen: extract from *The Institution of the Civil Service in the Third Reich, (1966)*; **pp.18, 19, 32** Adolf Hitler: extracts from *Mein Kampf, translated by Ralph Manheim (Hutchinson, 1969)*; **pp.20, 74** Joseph Goebbels: extracts from *Die Tagebucher von Joseph Goebbels, edited by E. Frohlich (K.S. Saur, 1993-2006)*; **p.20** W. Jochmann (editor): extract from *Nationalsozialismus und Revolution (1963)*; Ian Kershaw: **pp.33, 72, 77** extracts from *The 'Hitler Myth': Image and Reality (Clarendon Press, 1987)*; **p.58** extract from *Popular Opinion and Political Dissent in the Third Reich. Bavaria 1933–1945 (Oxford University Press, 1983)*; **p.119** extract from *Hitler, the Germans, and the Final Solution (Yale University Press, 2008)*; **p.126** extract from *The End: The Defiance and Destruction of Hitler's Germany 1944–1945 (The Penguin Press, 2011)*; **pp.52, 75** Max Domarus (editor): extracts from *Hitler, Speeches and Proclamations, 1932–1945 (1988)*; **p.57** Robert Gellately: extract from *Backing Hitler: Consent and Coercion in Nazi Germany (Oxford University Press, 2001)*; **p.59** Klaus-Michael Mallmann and Gerhard Paul: extract from *Herrschaft und Alltag, Ein Industriervier in 3rd Reich, (1991)*; **p.61** C.Hinton and J. Hite: extract from *Weimar and Nazi Germany (Hodder Education, 2000)*; **p.63** R. Eilers: extract from *Die Nationalsozialistische Schulpolitik, 1963)*; **p.61** J. Noakes and G. Pridham (editors): extracts from *Nazism 1919–1945, Volume 2: State, Economy and Society 1933–39 (A Documentary Reader) (Liverpool University Press, 2000)*; **p.63** Herman Rauschning: extract from *Hitler Speaks (Thornton Butterworth, 1939)*; **p.66** Sigrid Grabner and Hendrik Roder: extract from *Emmi Bonhoeffer (Lukas Verlag, 2004)*; **pp.70–71** extracts from *Letters to Hitler (Polity Press: 2011). Edited by Victoria Harris. English editor of the original German Briefe an Hitler (ed. Henrik Eberle)*.**p.72** Otto Dietrich: extract from *Hitler (H. Regnery Company, 1955)*; **p.76** Guenter Lewy: extract from *The Catholic Church and Nazi Germany (Da Capo Press, 2000)*; **p.92** Alan Milward: extract from *War, Economy and Society, 1939–1945 (Allen Lane, 1977)*; **p.92** R.J. Overy: extract from *War and Economy in the Third Reich (Clarendon Press, 1995)*; **p.92** Alan Tooze: extract from *The Wages of Destruction: The Making and Breaking of Nazi Germany (Allen Lane, 2006)*; **p. 95** Ulrich Herbert: extract from *Hitler's Foreign Workers (Cambridge University Press, 1997)*; **p.104** Nikolaus Wachsman: extract from *Hitler's Prisons (Yale University Press, 2004)*. **p.108** Beth A. Griech-Pollele: extract from *Bishop von Galen: German Catholicism and National Socialism (Yale University Press, 2002)*; **pp.109, 114, 132, 135** R.J. Evans: extracts from *The Third Reich at War (The Penguin Press, 2009)*; **p.109** H. Groscurth: extract from *Tagebucher eines Abwehroffiziers*; **p. 110** Zygmunt Klukowski: extract from *Diary from the Years of Occupation, 1933–44 (University of Illinois Press, 1993)*; **p.117** M. Broszat: extract from *Nationalistische Polenpolitik*; **p.120** Gitta Sereny: extract from *Into That Darkness: An Examination of Conscience (Vintage Books, 1974)*; **p.136** Anthony Beevor: extract from *The Fall of Berlin 1945 (Penguin Books, 2003)*; **p.136** Mathilde Wolff-Monckeberg: extract from *On the Other Side: To My Children: From Germany 1940–45*.

The Schools History Project

Set up in 1972 to bring new life to history for students aged 13–16, the Schools History Project continues to play an innovatory role in secondary an important contribution to make to the education of a young person. It does this by creating courses and materials which both respect the importance of up-to-date, well-researched history and provide enjoyable learning experiences for students.

Since 1978 the Project has been based at Trinity and All Saints University College Leeds. It continues to support, inspire and challenge teachers through the annual conference, regional courses and website: http://www.schoolshistoryproject.org.uk. The Project is also closely involved with government bodies and awarding bodies in the planning of courses for Key Stage 3, GCSE and A level.

For teacher support material for this title, visit www.schoolshistoryproject.org.uk.

Orders: please contact Bookpoint Ltd, 130 Milton Park, Abingdon, Oxon OX14 4SB. Telephone: +44 (0)1235 827720. Fax: +44 (0)1235 400454. Lines are open 9.00a.m.–5.00p.m., Monday to Saturday, with a 24-hour message answering service. Visit our website at www.hoddereducation.co.uk.

First published in 2013 by
Hodder Education,
an Hachette UK company
338 Euston Road
London NW1 3BH

Impression number 10 9 8 7 6 5 4 3 2 1

Year 2017 2016 2015 2014 2013

Typeset in ITC Usherwook Book 10pt by DC Graphic Design Ltd, Swanley Village, Kent.
Artwork by Barking Dog
Printed and bound in Italy

A catalogue record for this title is available from the British Library

ISBN 978 1 4441 7877 7

Contents

1 Nazi Germany: The essentials

Can you remember the highlight or your life the year you were nine? Alfons Heck was nine in 1938. It was a year full of special events for him, but one moment burned brightest in his memory: the day Adolf Hitler looked him in the eye.

Alfons lived his early life in the town of Wittlich in western Germany where he was raised on a farm by his grandparents. When he was very young, his parents moved to a nearby city with his twin brother. They were trying to set up a grocery store there but they knew it would be difficult. The German economy – like so many of the world's economies – was struggling at that time. They decided that Alfons would be one mouth too many to feed and decided to leave him behind.

On the farm, Alfons devoutly followed the Roman Catholic faith of his grandparents. In April 1933 he started school. His teacher was a member of the Nazi Party whose leader, Adolf Hitler, had just been made Chancellor of Germany. This Nazi government became part of his life as Alfons grew up. He later recalled how the local priest, when leading the school children in worship, would stand tall and declare '*Heil Hitler*!' before he led them in the Lord's Prayer. His grandparents never actually joined the Nazi Party but Alfons remembered how they admired Hitler for creating jobs for the millions who had been unemployed when he came to power in 1933. They also were grateful for Nazi policies that favoured farmers as their own prosperity grew steadily in the 1930s.

In April 1938, on Adolf Hitler's birthday, young Alfons was given a special privilege: he was allowed to join the junior section of the Hitler Youth (see page 64). The usual age of entry was ten, but Alfons was proud to be accepted a few months early. He was especially proud later that summer when his section of the Hitler Youth took part in the official opening of a new army base near his home town. This base showed how Hitler despised the Treaty of Versailles of 1919. Following Germany's defeat in the First World War this treaty had imposed a limit on the size of the army. But, by 1938, Hitler was openly breaking the treaty, rebuilding the armed forces and joining Germany and Austria together in one Greater Germany.

Hitler was not universally popular. Alfons remembered a rare visit in 1938 from his father who showed open contempt for Hitler and warned that his policies would lead to a war that would kill them all. Alfons heard his grandmother urging her son to keep quiet, for fear that he would be sent to one of the new concentration camps where opponents of the Nazis were already being imprisoned.

The young boy's greatest moment of 1938 came in the city of Nuremberg. From all the Hitler Youth of his locality, Alfons was selected to attend the Nazi Party rally that met there each year. On the opening night he found himself in the front row, barely forty feet from the Führer, Adolf Hitler.

△ **Adolf Hitler addresses the Nuremberg Youth Rally in September 1938. Somewhere in the front row stands the young Alfons Heck.**

The theme of the rally was 'Greater Germany'. In the opening event, Hitler chose to address the young people directly. He spoke of his own childhood hardships and of the despair of fighting as a young man in the trenches of the Great War only for Germany to be defeated and then humiliated by the peace treaty. But, he promised, things would be different for the young Germans before him. As he spoke he fixed his eyes on them and nine-year-old Alfons Heck felt the power of the Führer's direct gaze. 'You, my youth' urged Hitler, 'never forget that one day you will rule the world.'

Alfons returned to the farm more committed than ever to the Nazi cause. In the months that followed, he witnessed the Jewish people of his home town being beaten and their stores trashed by truck loads of young Nazis who had driven into Wittlich one November day. In the first months of 1939 he saw the increasing number of troops in the nearby army garrison. Then, on 1 September 1939, he woke to the sound of the radio that, most unusually, had been turned on at breakfast time. It carried the news that German armed forces had invaded Poland. Within days another world war had started.

During the war Alfons became a senior leader in the Hitler Youth. In the final months, aged 16, he was manning an anti-aircraft battery defending the skies over his home town. When the war was lost, amidst the starvation and ruins of Germany, he was captured and held in a prisoner of war camp. There, he was shown film of the death camps where millions of Jews and others had been murdered. After his release in 1946, he made his way back to Nuremberg, the city where he had once been captivated by the charisma of Adolf Hitler. This time he went to stand outside the courtroom as loudspeakers relayed the evidence against leading Nazis on trial for war crimes. He was learning the awful realities of Nazi Germany. And yet, looking back, he recalled:

> I never once during the Hitler years thought of myself as anything but a decent, honourable, young German, blessed with a glorious future.

This book takes you through those same 'Hitler years'. Maybe, with hindsight, you will understand the events and powerful forces of the time in ways that Alfons Heck, caught up in the midst of them, could not.

You may be wondering how we know about Alfons Heck. In 1951 he emigrated to Canada, married and moved on to the USA in 1963. After working as a bus driver, he became involved in sharing the early experiences of his life with children and students to show how Germans like him had been captivated by the Nazis. His autobiography *A Child of Hitler* was published in 1985. He died in 2005.

Germany 1933–45

You have just met Alfons Heck, a young German who lived through the Hitler years. Starting with one person's experience is a powerful way to get to grips with the past but it also helps to stand well back and take in the bigger picture. That is what the timeline on these pages aims to do. The individual enquiries in this book will explore the main issues, but this spread is your 'satnav' across time – so you can see where you're going. You'll see that the big timeline of the years of Nazi government tapers off at each end. German history did not start with Hitler's coming to power, nor did it end with his death. To understand the impact of Nazi rule on the German people you need to know what happened before 1933.

1918

First World War ends; Weimar Republic begins

1933

January: Hitler becomes Chancellor of Germany
February: Reichstag fire
March: First concentration camp set up, at Dachau
March: Enabling Act
April: All Jews banned from civil service
April: SA lead boycott of Jewish shops
May: Trade unions banned
July: All other political parties banned

1934

June: Night of the Long Knives
August: Hindenburg dies; Hitler becomes President as well as Chancellor

1935

March: Compulsory military service introduced
September: Nuremberg Laws

193[6]

August: Berlin Olympics

1943

February: German Army surrenders at Stalingrad

1944

June: D-Day – allies land in France
July: Bomb plot fails to kill Hitler

1945

April: Red Army enters Berlin. Hitler commits suicide
May: Germany surrenders

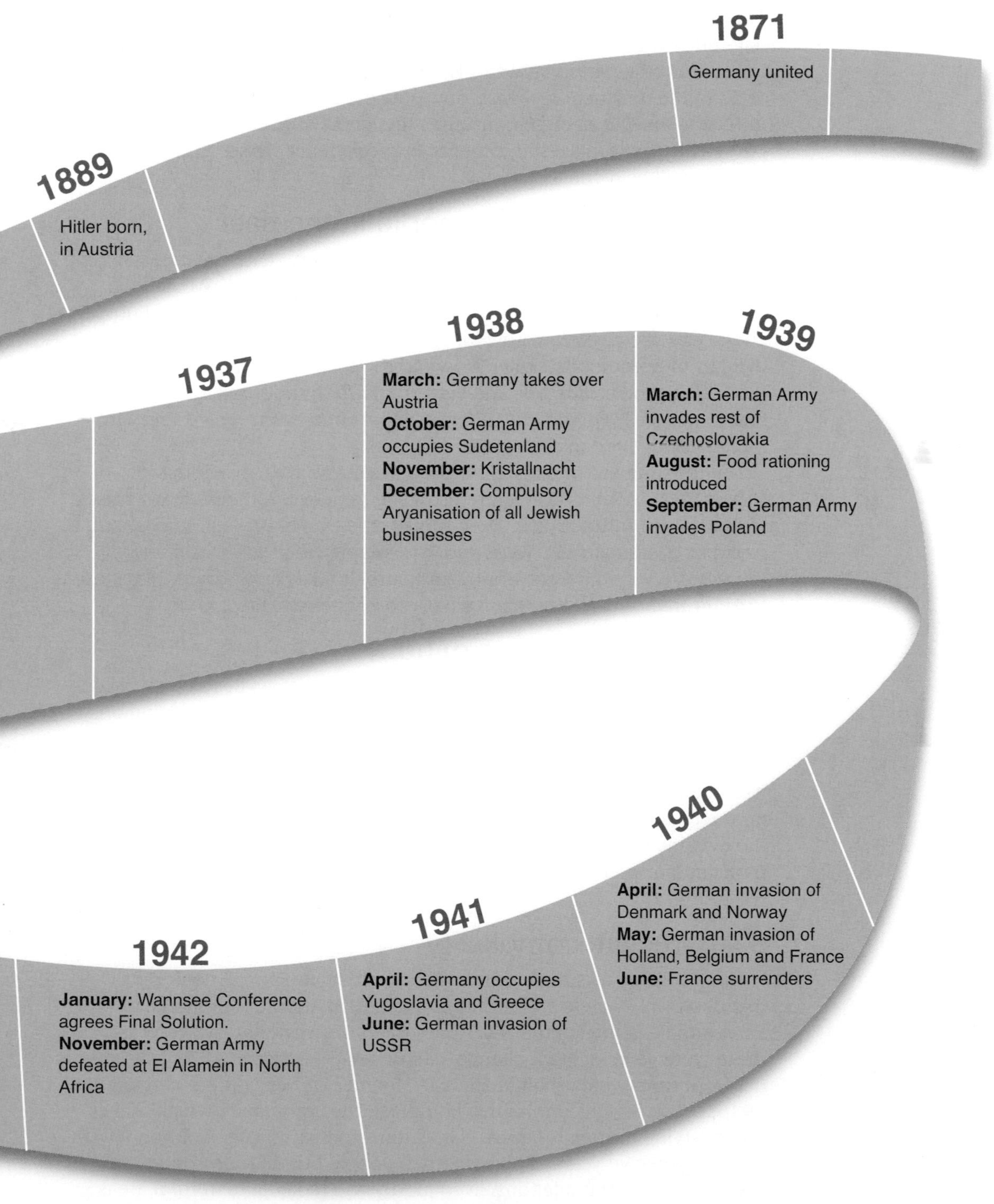
1871
Germany united
1889
Hitler born, in Austria
1937
1938
March: Germany takes over Austria
October: German Army occupies Sudetenland
November: Kristallnacht
December: Compulsory Aryanisation of all Jewish businesses
1939
March: German Army invades rest of Czechoslovakia
August: Food rationing introduced
September: German Army invades Poland
1940
April: German invasion of Denmark and Norway
May: German invasion of Holland, Belgium and France
June: France surrenders
1941
April: Germany occupies Yugoslavia and Greece
June: German invasion of USSR
1942
January: Wannsee Conference agrees Final Solution.
November: German Army defeated at El Alamein in North Africa

What does this book try to do?

This book helps you develop a deep understanding of Nazi Germany. We have structured it around eight enquiry questions, each focusing on key issues from the period between Hitler becoming Chancellor in January 1933 to the destruction of Nazi power at the end of the Second World War in May 1945. Our book also includes 'Insights' which allow you to explore particular people, places and events in more depth. These Enquiries and Insights will help you to:

1 Enter the minds of people in the past

Historians try to explain big events. One of the problems we face in trying to explain Nazism is hindsight: we know how it all ended. We need to make a special effort to understand how the people of a modern European country, well-educated, with a long cultural tradition, could allow a racist dictator to become their ruler. How did they then allow him to stifle democracy and civil rights, and systematically murder millions of their fellow citizens? Why did they then take part in the war he led Germany into, causing them to die in their millions?

By the time you've finished this book you'll have learned that convincing explanations require us to see people, their ideas and actions, in their own time, not ours. Even though the events you will read about took place less than 100 years ago, the people who took part in them inhabited a very different world from ours. It takes an effort of imagination to enter their minds, but that's what good historians have to do.

2 Make up your own mind

Ever since the Nazis came to prominence in Germany, people have tried to explain how and why this happened and what exactly was going on. The arguments went on after the end of Nazism and still continue to this day. This book therefore invites you to enter into a dialogue which has been going on for some time. Each of the enquiry questions which make up the chapters of this book require you to reach judgements, based on the evidence. You will have to look beneath the surface of propaganda and partisan interpretations and make up your own mind about the issues you will address.

3 Appreciate complexity

History is rarely as simple as it looks at first sight. Every Enquiry in this book will suggest different layers of explanation or comparison. For example, although the Nazis only ruled Germany for twelve years, these were years of great change. Life under the Nazis in 1938 was very different from what it had been in 1933 and was very different again by 1945. Accounts which miss this point lack the complexity which makes for satisfying history. Nor were these, for the great majority of non-Jewish Germans, twelve years of abject terror; people put their personal lives first, made accommodations, lived 'under the radar'. Life in rural areas was different from what it was in the big cities, different in the north of Germany from the south. Only by taking on these complexities can you begin to reach a full understanding of this fascinating period.

Why is Nazi Germany worth studying?

Hitler's plans led eventually to the Second World War and the Holocaust. We are still living with the results of those cataclysmic events: the map of Europe was re-drawn after the war and two Super Powers emerged from the ruins. The Holocaust marked the beginning of the end of the unquestioned supremacy of European civilisation, with huge consequences for world history. It also demonstrated to the world for all time where ideas of racial superiority eventually lead.

The Germany in which Hitler became Chancellor was a democracy. You will discover that democracy can be fragile, and needs more than just a carefully-written constitution to make it strong. You will see how **civil rights** can be eroded and how far people can be manipulated.

Civil rights enable citizens of a state to be free, without suffering discrimination, to be able to vote and be treated equally in law.

This is a story of a modern dictatorship. Hitler was not the first, nor the last dictator. Nor are all dictators the same. But studying Hitler, his beliefs and policies, will help you comprehend how dictatorships arise. You will have to explain what he set out to do with his dictatorial power. You will discover how difficult dictators are to remove.

Some of you will have studied Nazi Germany before. If you have, you will now need to move up a gear, getting behind previous knowledge and seeking deeper, more complex, explanations.

If you have never studied this topic before: welcome! You're going to be amazed!

So is this the only book I need?

Definitely not! Never rely on just one book when studying history. Success at A level can only come by engaging with a range of texts that argue different points of view, or provide different levels of detail.

Which other books should you read? Ideally you will find books that have not just been written for A level, but ones that take you deeper. There are many excellent and fascinating books about Nazi Germany. You will find some suggestions at www.schoolshistoryproject.org.uk/Publishing/BooksSHP/Enquiring/NG/biblio.html.

◁ The authors of this book!

Most people probably expect historians to deliver 'the truth' about the past. But historians don't live on desert islands. They have their own standpoints, which are affected by the times and the places they live in. The next pages show some of the ways historians have tried to explain Nazi Germany in the years since 1945. You will come across their differing viewpoints several times as you read this book.

What do historians say about Nazi Germany?

You probably already have some questions about Nazi Germany which you want to find answers to. We hope that the Enquiries in this book will help you to find some of them. Historians have been working at providing answers to questions about Nazi Germany ever since 1945: what have they got to say and how were their ideas shaped by the times and places in which they were formed?

The Cold War context

Out of the chaos of the fall of Nazi Germany in 1945, two Super Powers emerged: the USA and the USSR. Although they worked together to defeat Hitler, they were rivals before the war. This rivalry soon re-emerged once the war was over and it lasted for the next 45 years. It was not just a military rivalry, but a rivalry of systems. The USA and its western allies were capitalist, liberal democracies – that is, industry and commerce were largely in private hands, while governments were decided by multi-party elections. The governments of the USSR and its allies were run by a single party, the Communist Party, based on the ideas of Karl Marx; all industry and commerce was controlled by the state.

The Cold War divided the whole world, not just Europe, but it was in Europe and especially in Germany, that the two Super Powers came face to face. By 1949 the former US, British and French occupied zones of Germany had become the new Federal Republic of Germany, known as West Germany, while the eastern, Soviet zone became the new German Democratic Republic, known as East Germany. Berlin was itself divided and in 1962 a wall was built right across the city.

This War was 'cold' because there was hardly any direct conflict between the two sides. It was a war of propaganda over two systems in which historians took part. Rival explanations of Nazi Germany's history were significant: was Nazi Germany a capitalist state, in which case its origins and its heirs were in the west? Or was it a one party totalitarian dictatorship, in which case its true heirs were in the east?

East German, Marxist historians

Karl Marx had argued that power always lies with the class which wields economic power. Marxist historians therefore explained Hitler's rise to power by pointing to his close links with German capitalists. Several key industrialists supported the Nazi Party in its early years. Iron and steel, chemical and electrical companies were rewarded with lucrative contracts when Hitler carried out his massive rearmament programme. The forced labour camps set up by the Nazis produced goods for private companies, such as IG Farben at Auschwitz.

These Marxist interpretations continued to dominate East German and Soviet accounts of Nazism throughout the Cold War period up to 1989.

West German historians

After the war, some West German historians pointed to the history of German militarism and desire for conquest. Hitler's own ambitions, and then achievements, were therefore very beguiling to the German people. Others emphasised how alien Hitler and Nazism were to Germany. Hitler's racism came from Austria, his nationalism from France, his Social Darwinism (see page 102) from Britain. He was therefore an aberration in German history, which could now return to its 'true' course.

Western historians, 1945–1960s

American and British historians in the years immediately after 1945 assumed that most of the records of the Nazi era had been destroyed in the last years of the war. Certainly, with Germany in chaos, access to archives was difficult. They therefore based their accounts heavily on the testimony of witnesses at the Nuremberg War Crime Trials, 1945–46. They drew a picture of a country led by a maniacal Hitler. His intentions were clear from the start, including the Holocaust, and he set about fulfilling them as soon as he was in power. The German people were under the total control of the Nazis, with a huge army of Gestapo spies (see page 57) suppressing all individual freedoms. Hannah Arendt described in 1958 how totalitarian government worked:

'a system of ubiquitous spying, where everybody might be a police agent and each individual finds himself under constant surveillance.'

So complete was this control that ordinary Germans knew nothing about Nazi atrocities or the Holocaust.

Western historians, 1960s–1980s

The 1960s was a time of rejection of the certainties of the post-war period, in historiography as well as fashion and pop music. Historians of Nazi Germany, beginning to come to grips with the archives of the Nazi years, began to tell some very different stories.

Far from being in total control, Hitler's management of power was haphazard, subject to modification by the structures he had to work within. Hans Mommsen wrote that Hitler was:

'unwilling to take decisions, frequently uncertain, exclusively concerned with upholding his prestige and personal authority, influenced by his entourage.' (1966) He was, in other words, 'a weak dictator'.

Historians also began to question the view that the German people were totally suppressed. Signs of dissent and even of criticism of extreme Nazi anti-Semitism such as *Kristallnacht* (see page 115), were recorded in Martin Broszat's study of the impact of Nazi rule in rural Bavaria (the Bavaria Project, 1977–1983).

From the 1980s

Further detailed studies flowed from historians' work on specific sources: groups of workers, individual towns, particular Gestapo officers and individual biographies, for example. They replaced the earlier 'black and white' picture of villainous Nazis and innocent German victims, with shades of grey. Historians showed that many Germans had supported the Nazis, most notably the anti-democratic 'old élites', still powerful in Weimar Germany. Many others simply reached an accommodation with the Nazis, to keep their jobs, or even to gain personal advantage. It was also clear that the Gestapo was not all-powerful and that many Germans actually approved of their targeting of gay men, habitual criminals, tramps and the work-shy.

The Germans could not have been totally ignorant of Nazi forced labour, deportations and the Holocaust itself. In *Hitler's Willing Executioners* (1996) Daniel Goldhagen argued that ordinary German policemen took part in killing Jews in Poland. Broszat argued that the Nazis were not an aberration, but in several ways a continuation of trends in German history.

2 Who were the Germans and what were their hopes and fears?

■ This is a light-touch opening enquiry, designed to help you get used to 'reading with a purpose'. All you must do is to work through each of the key events that follow, simply recording, in a few sentences, the range of hopes and fears that might have been held by people in Germany in the 1930s.

There were 50 million people living in Germany by 1933. Some lived in enormous modern cities, some in tiny remote villages. There were men and women, young and old, rich and poor, farmers and factory-workers, artists and engineers, Protestants, Roman Catholics and Jews.

In the years just before Hitler came to power, these people had lived through many historic and dramatic events. Their responses to these events and how they thought about them in retrospect, helped to shape their choices as new situations unfolded before them.

To help you understand the complex context in which Hitler rose to power in Germany, these pages show eight key images, moments or developments from the recent past of every adult German. Viewpoints might differ, but no one could escape the influence of these historic memories.

Memory 1: Kaiser Wilhelm II and the Second Empire

Many Germans in 1933 would have looked at the photograph opposite with pride and nostalgia. From 1871 to 1918 Germany was known as 'the Second Empire' (the first being the medieval Holy Roman Empire based predominantly in German lands). This Second Empire was a military autocracy ruled by the Kaiser (Emperor) and his unelected advisers, chosen from the senior ranks of the army and aristocratic Prussian landowners. The powerful and successful army was virtually a 'state within a state', almost completely outside democratic control. German society was orderly, with class distinctions that no one was expected to cross. The churches (60 per cent Protestant and 40 per cent Roman Catholic) had their own hierarchies. From the pulpit and through their control of education they promoted deference to those in power. There was a parliament, the Reichstag, but it had little power and the ruling class did not hide their contempt for democracy. These were the men who took Germany into the First World War.

Other Germans would have looked at this photo with loathing. The German ruling class still saw their country as a land of peasants and landowners. In fact, it was becoming a highly industrialised nation – nearly 50 per cent of the population worked in industry by 1914. Many thousands belonged to the powerful trade union movement and to the German Socialist Party which, despite government harassment, was the largest in the world. It was the largest party in the Reichstag, but was always excluded from power. Therefore, Germans with **leftist** views would regard the people in the photo as class enemies or, at least, as a barrier that prevented Germany becoming the liberal democracy they wanted.

In political terms, the **left** refers to those with socialist or communist views. The **right** refers to those with conservative, often nationalist views.

▷ Kaiser Wilhelm and some of his generals in January, 1914.

Memory 2: Workers uprisings, November 1918 to January 1919

In the closing weeks of the First World War, armed risings erupted in Berlin, Munich and other cities. For German Communists, these uprising should have led to their revolution, emulating the October Revolution in Russia only a year before. For German nationalists, whose loyalties lay with the Second Empire, the Kaiser and the Imperial Army, these uprisings explained their defeat in 1918: mutineers and left-wingers 'stabbed the army in the back', by starting a revolution at home, making it impossible for the army to go on fighting.

In fact, it had been clear to army generals that Germany was facing defeat from the late summer of 1918. In September they advised the Kaiser to bring the Social Democrats into government, who would then take the blame for the inevitable disaster. Sailors in Kiel mutinied in October, and workers' risings began in November. The Kaiser fled to Holland on 10 November 1918, but his advisers and generals stayed behind to promulgate the 'stab in the back' myth, letting themselves off the hook.

With Berlin in chaos, the new government had to meet in the town of Weimar, which is why the system of government in Germany from 1919 to 1933 was named the 'Weimar Republic'. The Communist revolution was only crushed when the Weimar government, led by the Social Democrats, used demobilised soldiers against them. Many of the Communists' comrades were killed. The result was lasting hostility between the two parties of the left – the Communists and Social Democrats.

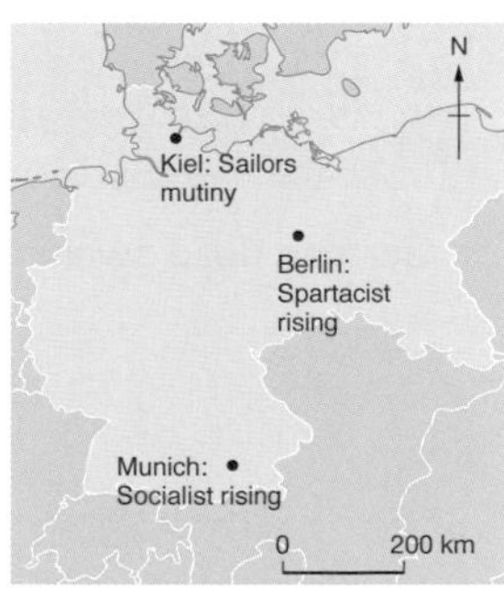

△ Uprisings in Germany, 1918.

■ How would Memories 1 and 2 affect German hopes and fears in the years afterwards? Record your views in a few sentences.

Memory 3: Defeat in 1918

△ German dead awaiting burial in Memel in March 1915.

■ How would Memory 3 affect German hopes and fears in the years afterwards? Record your views in a few sentences.

In 1918, despite all the promises that the war would bring victory and prosperity, the army that the German people had been taught to admire and adore was facing defeat. By then, 2 million Germans had been killed and 4.2 million wounded. There were mutinies in the German Imperial Fleet at Kiel and in some army units on the Western Front just at the time when revolutions broke out in German cities. Faced with uprisings at home, their forces in retreat and the prospect of a humiliating defeat, Germany sued for peace. An Armistice was declared on 11 November 1918.

The timing of this ceasefire meant that German civilians never witnessed the war on their own territory – Germany was never invaded. The sudden and largely unexpected defeat made it hard for them to come to terms with what followed at the peace conference in Paris in 1919. There, the victorious Allies (led by Britain, France and the USA) decided what should happen to Germany. The shock of defeat was followed by the humiliation of the peace settlement.

Memory 4: The Treaty of Versailles, 1919

When the German leaders agreed to an armistice in November 1918, they were hopeful that they would take part in a negotiated treaty based on the 'Fourteen Points' published by US President Woodrow Wilson. These sought to prevent further wars by avoiding revengeful terms, by giving all nationalities the opportunity to rule themselves and by mutual disarmament. Unfortunately Lloyd George and Clemenceau, the representatives of Britain and France, had other views. Clemenceau particularly, having seen Germany invade his country twice in his lifetime, even wanted to 'disunite' Germany, splitting it up again as it was back in 1815 (see Memory 5, below).

Instead of a negotiated treaty, the Weimar government was faced with a dictated peace – a '*diktat*'. They were told that if they did not sign, the war would re-start and their country would certainly be invaded.

These were the main terms of the Treaty as they emerged from tough negotiations:

- Armaments. The German Army was restricted to 100,000 men and conscription was forbidden. All its weapons, including tanks, were to be destroyed. The navy was to be restricted to 36 ships. German armed forces were not to include submarines, or any aircraft.
- Territory. Germany lost territory to France, Belgium, Denmark and Poland. The Rhineland was to be de-militarised (these changes are shown on the maps in Memory 5). All Germany's colonies were taken over by the League of Nations, who handed them over to be governed by League members.
- Blame. Article 231 stated that Germany had to accept complete responsibility for starting the war.
- Reparations. As they were to blame, Germany had to pay reparations to the Allies to compensate them for the destruction and losses caused by the war. The sum for reparations was fixed later at £6.6 million.

In Germany, the reaction to the Treaty was outrage and anger. Most of this was aimed at the Weimar government, even though they had no choice but to sign. The Weimar politicians had to accept blame for the war, even though they had had no say in the events of 1914. Reparations would burden an already crippled economy for many years. The Treaty of Versailles reverberated through German history for years to come.

■ How would Memory 4 affect German hopes and fears in the years afterwards? Record your views in a few sentences.

Memory 5: The shrinking of German territory in 1919

England has been unified since the tenth century, and the United Kingdom has existed for over 300 years, its territory unchanged. The history of Germany has been very different, and much less stable, as these three maps reveal.

Map 1: The states of Germany in 1815

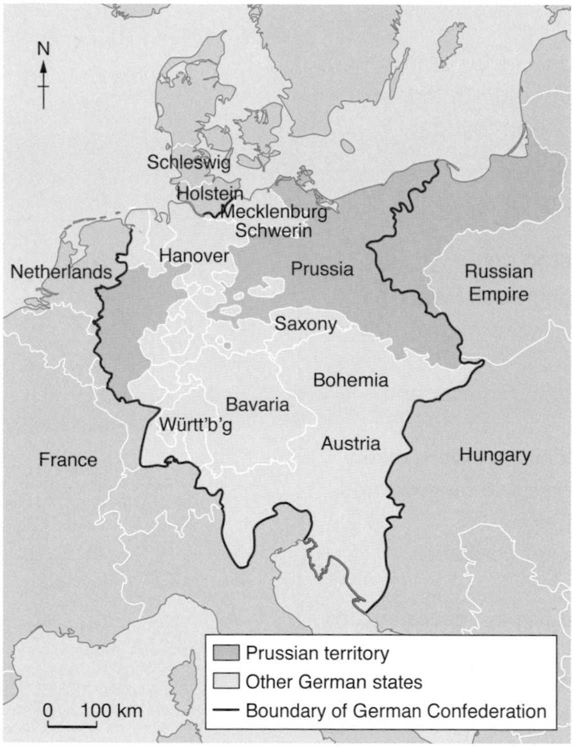

Germany was not a country in 1815. There were in fact 39 independent states and cities, varying enormously in size and traditions, united only by their common language and a loose confederation. By far the most powerful states were Prussia, whose territory, as you can see, included lands in the east and the west and Austria, whose territories included lands which were not German at all.

Map 2: Imperial Germany, 1871–1919

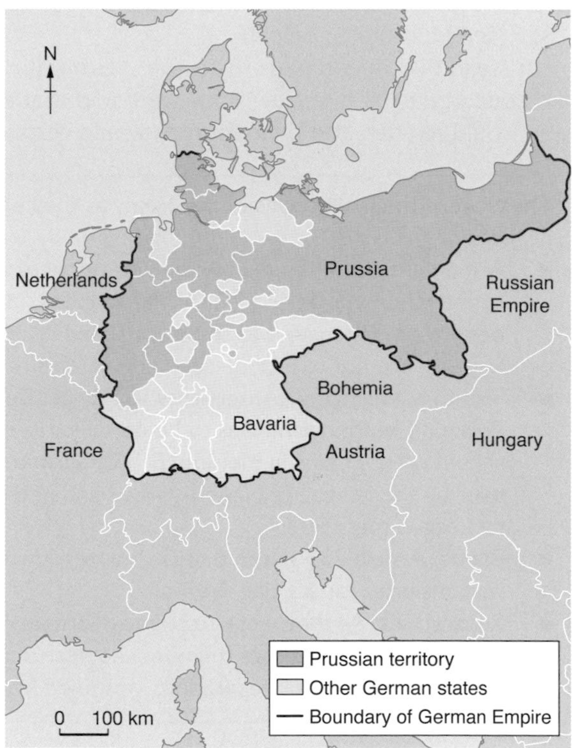

One of the lasting legacies of the French Revolution was nationalism. This was felt in Germany as an overwhelming desire to become a single powerful European nation. This was largely achieved through the efficient, well-armed Prussian Army. Following crushing victories over Denmark in 1864, Austria in 1866 and France in 1870–71, a united federal Germany was created. King Wilhelm of Prussia became the first kaiser (emperor) of Germany in 1871. His grandson was Kaiser Wilhelm II (see pages 10 and 11).

This map is therefore an expression of successful German nationhood, achieved through military success.

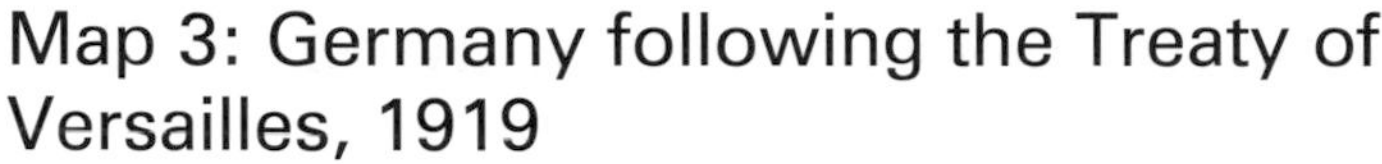

Map 3: Germany following the Treaty of Versailles, 1919

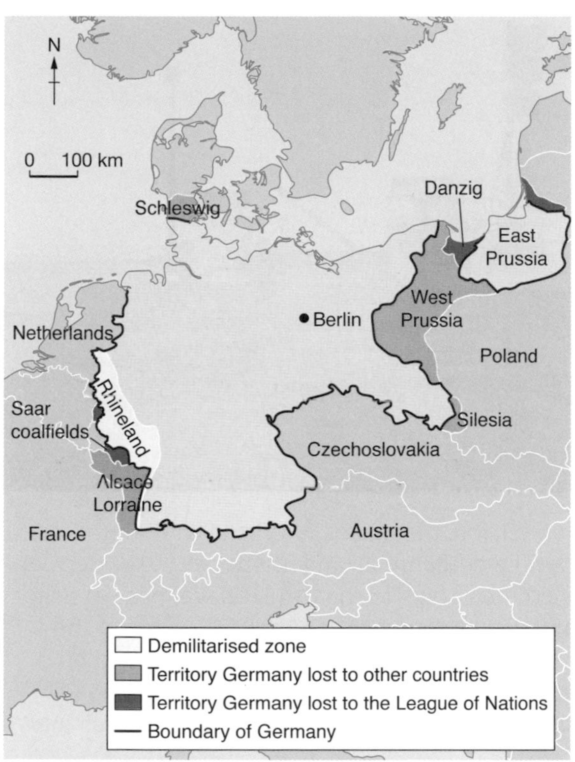

As we have seen, several of the terms of the Treaty of Versailles were regarded with shame, loathing and anger by many Germans. The territorial losses that Germany had to suffer seemed particularly designed to humiliate their nation, to rob them of their pride in its military history.

a) Part of Schleswig, gained by Germany after the war with Denmark in 1864, had to be returned.

b) Alsace and Lorraine, gained by Germany after the war with France in 1870–71, had to be returned.

c) East Prussia became detached from the rest of Germany by creating the 'free city' of Danzig and by giving a swathe of territory to Poland, so that this newly created nation – regarded with contempt by German nationalists – had access to the Baltic Sea.

The changes shown in these three maps meant that elderly Germans in the 1930s would have seen the borders of their homeland extend and shrink several times in their lifetime. There were now Germans in parts of Europe who did not live in Germany itself. The implications of this were that, while it was fairly clear what it meant to be British at this time, there was no clear and settled German national boundary or identity in the first half of the twentieth century. Few Germans would be surprised at the thought of their borders being redrawn once more – and some would actively work to achieve exactly that.

■ How would Memory 5 affect German hopes and fears in the years afterwards? Record your views in a few sentences.

Memory 6: The scuttling of the German fleet, June 1919

▷ German battleship scuttled at Scapa Flow in 1919.

This image would conjure up terrible memories for virtually all Germans, whatever their beliefs. Under the ceasefire arrangements in 1918, German naval commanders had sailed their ships to the British naval base at Scapa Flow to the north of Scotland. When they learned that the terms of the Treaty of Versailles would restrict the German navy to just 36 ships, of which only 6 could be battleships, these commanders deliberately sank or 'scuttled' their ships as an act of defiance rather than let them fall into British hands.

Memory 7: The hyperinflation of 1923

This was another terrible recent memory for all Germans. Economic revival after the war was slow for many countries but especially so for Germany. In addition to this, Germany had to pay reparations as part of the Treaty of Versailles. This amounted to 10 per cent of German wealth leaving the country. In 1923, Germany failed to pay the reparations instalment which led to French and Belgian troops occupying the Ruhr, the heart of German industry. The government ordered workers to go on strike and paid them, together with compensation to companies for lost income. They did not have the money for this, but they did have printing presses, so they printed it, as banknotes of increasingly high values.

Some of the images from this period of hyperinflation might seem funny to us: kites made of banknotes, housewives burning notes in their cooking stoves. But it was not funny really. Prices rose so fast that employees were paid every other day, but they never had enough to live on. Many starved and infant mortality rose. For those on fixed incomes, it was a catastrophe: the careful savings of a lifetime were spent buying food for a couple of days. Not everyone lost: those living on borrowed money found it easy to clear their debts. A new currency, the Rentenmark, restored financial order in 1924, but the memory remained of the old German values of thrift and order being turned upside down.

For this, too, the Weimar government was blamed.

■ How would Memories 6 and 7 affect German hopes and fears in the years afterwards? Record your views in a few sentences.

Memory 8: The birth of modernism in Berlin in the 1920s

△ Nikolaus Braun, *Berlin Street Scene* (1921).

This painting would appeal to many Germans who relished the opportunity to put the heavy hand of the Kaiser's Germany behind them and embrace all that was modern and new. Berlin, with its vibrant street life, its bustling coffee shops, its fashionable women, its artistic experiment, its jazz clubs and its liberated attitude to sex was the most exciting city in Europe. The city stood for all that was radical about the Weimar Republic, with votes and equal rights for all men and women.

Many other Germans hated modern art like Braun's painting. They also hated the liberated, modern Germany exemplified by Berlin. A journalist, Wilhelm Stapel, writing in 1927, called it 'The cesspool of the republic'. He went on: 'All too many Slavs and all too many uninhibited east European Jews have been mixed into the population of Berlin.' (The casually open racist language used by Stapel here was all too common.)

Amongst those who expressed revulsion at modernist culture and above all at the unwelcome influence of the Jews in German society was the man who was to dominate German history from 1933 to 1945: Adolf Hitler.

■ By now you should have quite a few examples of the diverse hopes and fears of the German people in the early 1930s. How do you think they will influence Germany's future?

Mein Kampf – Adolf Hitler's early years

In 1925, Volume I of a new book went on sale in Germany. *Mein Kampf* (My Struggle) was written by a largely unknown Austrian named Adolf Hitler. The book's rambling mixture of autobiography and political testament revealed the personal obsessions of the man who went on to shape German and world history between 1933 and 1945.

Hitler was born in 1889 into a poor family in Braunau am Inn on Austria's border with Germany: the man who became the Führer of Germany was not even born a German citizen. But in *Mein Kampf* he recalled how, as a child, he read about the mighty new state of Germany that arose from the Franco-Prussian war of 1870–71 and how he asked himself ...

> Is there a difference ... between the Germans who fought that war and the other Germans? Why did not Austria also take part in it? Why did not my father and all the others fight in that struggle? Are we not the same as the other Germans? Do we not all belong together?

By the age of eighteen Hitler's parents had died and he was living in Vienna, capital of the sprawling Austro-Hungarian Empire. Hitler lived in cheap hostels, scraping a living as an artist, painting careful, lifeless sketches of the city. His obsession with the supremacy of the German people was fuelled by his distaste for the city's immigrants drawn in from non-German lands that had been ruled by the Austrian emperors for hundreds of years. Hitler hated this multi-ethnic mix and picked up the rabid anti-Semitism which was rife in the city. In *Mein Kampf*, Hitler wrote that Vienna was filled with ...

> Czechs, Poles, Hungarians, Ruthenians, Serbs and Croats, etc, and always that bacillus which is the solvent of human society, the Jew, here and there and everywhere – the whole spectacle was repugnant to me. The gigantic city seemed to be the incarnation of mongrel depravity.

Hitler used to keep warm by sitting in the public gallery in the Austrian Parliament. He despised what he saw as the weakness of endless debating that marked multi-party politics:

> A turbulent mass of people, all gesticulating and bawling against one another, with a pathetic old man shaking his bell and making frantic efforts to call the House to a sense of its dignity by friendly appeals, exhortations, and grave warnings. I could not refrain from laughing. ... [After] a year of such observation ... I recognised that the institution itself was wrong in its very essence and form.

At the same time as he lost all faith in parliamentary democracy, Hitler developed a particular loathing for Austria's left wing Social Democratic Party whose leadership, he believed, was under the control of Jews. On moving to Germany in 1913, he found that the Social Democrats there formed the biggest party in the German Reichstag, fuelled by the votes of workers from Germany's growing industrial cities. Although he despised their socialist views, Hitler admired the effectiveness of Social Democrat speeches and propaganda and followed their example in years to come.

When the First World War broke out in August 1914, Hitler immediately joined the German Army where this rather lonely and unsuccessful man found instant close comradeship and a sense of patriotic purpose. He was decorated with the Iron Cross, First Class, on the recommendation of a Jewish officer. Gassed in 1918, Hitler was convalescing when the war ended. The news of Germany's defeat drove him into a frenzy:

> So it had all been in vain. In vain all the sacrifices and privations; in vain the hours in which, with mortal fear clutching at our hearts, we nevertheless did our duty; in vain the death of two million who died. Had they died for this? Did all this happen only so that a gang of wretched criminals could lay hands on the Fatherland?

Along with millions of Germans Hitler accepted the 'stab in the back' myth (see page 11) that Germany could still have won the war had it not been for the Social Democrats, Communists and Jews. On returning to Munich in November 1918, still serving as a soldier, he learned that army commanders had decided to resist the spread of Communism by indoctrinating their troops with right-wing, nationalist, anti-Semitic views. Hitler eagerly joined this programme first as a student, then as a trainer. These were the first steps in his political career. In *Mein Kampf* he described how he soon discovered his talent as a political speaker.

> I took up my work with the greatest delight and devotion ... I was now able to confirm ... that I had a talent for public speaking ... No task could have been more pleasing to me than this one ... During the course of my lectures I have led back hundreds and even thousands of my fellow countrymen to their people and their fatherland.

When, in June 1919, he learned about the crushing terms of the Treaty of Versailles (see page 13) Hitler called it 'a scandal and a disgrace ... an act of highway robbery against our people'. His anger festered in the confused, bitter years after the war. He was not alone. Hundreds of extreme political parties sprang up in Germany.

Working as an army spy, Hitler visited the tiny German Workers Party in September 1919 and within a few days he had become a member. He admired its commitment to German nationalism and its desire to appeal to the masses. But above all it gave him a stage to express his own views and a chance to take over as leader when his skills as a speaker brought increasing numbers to meetings.

In February 1920 the party changed its name to become the National Socialist German Workers Party – or Nazi Party for short. By July, Hitler was the party leader. The Nazi Party had a 25 point programme that set out its hatred for Jews and Communists, its determination to overthrow the terms of the Treaty of Versailles, and a commitment to create a new, greater Germany joining all Germans in one state and taking land in the east so that it could feed its people.

In *Mein Kampf*, Hitler described the meeting where he first detected signs of mass support ...

> As the masses streamed towards the exits, ... I knew that a movement was now set afoot among the German people ... A fire was kindled from whose glowing heat the sword would be fashioned which would restore freedom to the German people and bring back life to the German nation ... The Goddess of Vengeance was now getting ready to redress the treason of the 9th of November, 1918.

On 8 November 1923 Hitler and armed Nazi Stormtroopers tried but failed to take over the government in Munich by force. This became known as the 'Munich Putsch'. He was arrested and put on trial. A sympathetic judge gave him a relatively light sentence, to be served in a large, comfortable room at Landsberg Castle. It was in his nine months there that Hitler wrote *Mein Kampf*. This photograph was taken as the dishevelled, angry author left prison in 1924. His political career seemed to be over. But, within ten years the Austrian-born, ex-army corporal had become Chancellor (Prime Minister) of Germany. It was a remarkable and fateful transformation.

△ **Adolf Hitler leaving Landsberg Castle.**

3 Chancellor through his own efforts?

△ Adolf Hitler, former corporal, now Chancellor of Germany, bows his head to President Hindenburg, former Field Marshal, 30 January 1933.

On 30 January 1933, Adolf Hitler, former army corporal, accepted the invitation of President Hindenberg to become Chancellor of Germany. That evening, the appointment of their leader was acclaimed by Nazis with triumphant street processions. In Berlin, the torch-lit march, with swastika flags waving, was ecstatically recorded in his diary by Hitler's propaganda chief, Joseph Göbbels:

> Great jubilation. Down there the people are creating an uproar ... The torches come. It starts at 7 o'clock. Endless. Till 10 o'clock ... 12 o'clock. Awakening! Indescribable. Prepare the election campaign. The last.

The police, who in theory were politically neutral, shone a searchlight on the window where President Hindenburg stood, and on Hitler, at the balcony of the house next door. A few days later, at a similar procession in Hamburg, Luise Solmitz, a young German teacher, reported:

> 20,000 **brownshirts** followed one another like waves in the sea, their faces shone with enthusiasm in the light of the torches. 'For our Leader, our Chancellor, Adolf Hitler a threefold Heil!' They sang 'The Republic is shit' ... They sang of the blood of the Jews which would squirt from their knives.

The '**brownshirts**' was the common name for the Stürm Abteilung (SA), the Stormtroopers, Nazi Party members and streetfighters, so-called from their uniform.

Hitler's appointment as Chancellor was an extraordinary development: the constitution of the German Weimar Republic was one of the most democratic in the world. Yet Hitler and Nazis did not hide their contempt for democracy – look above at what the Nazis were chanting in the streets of Hamburg, and see what Göbbels says about one 'last' election. Despite this, Hitler, a failure for most of his early life, an Austrian who only became a German citizen in 1932, had reached this pinnacle of power. But how had he achieved this? Was it entirely through his own efforts? Or did he just ride events as they took place?

Enquiry Focus: To what extent did Hitler become Chancellor through his own efforts?

This is your first full Enquiry. The pathway you will use to get into the topic is indicated by a question, a problem needing an answer. This is just how historians work, and it means that you have to read the pages that follow with a purpose. So, DON'T just start reading and making notes, pushing the question to the back of your mind. That way you end up with lots of notes, but no answers. DO think about the question as you read and gradually put together your response.

Always begin by looking carefully at the question. This Enquiry is a kind of explanation question exploring the reasons why Hitler was invited to become Chancellor of Germany in January, 1933. The key phrase in the full question above is 'to what extent'. As you work through the Enquiry, you will consider seven factors that helped Hitler gain power. They are shown on the diagram below. When you have read through the section on each factor we will ask you to:

1. Summarise in your written notes HOW the factor contributed to Hitler becoming Chancellor in one or two sentences.
2. Decide HOW FAR Hitler was responsible for either creating or exploiting that factor.
3. Show what you have decided by placing the appropriate factor number on a large copy of the diagram. Place the number near to the central box if you believe that factor was due very largely to his own efforts, or further away if you judge that the factor owed little or nothing to his own efforts (or was not down to him at all).
4. Add a sentence to your notes to justify where you have placed the factor number.

At the end of the enquiry we will prompt you to revise your hypothesis and finalise your answer.

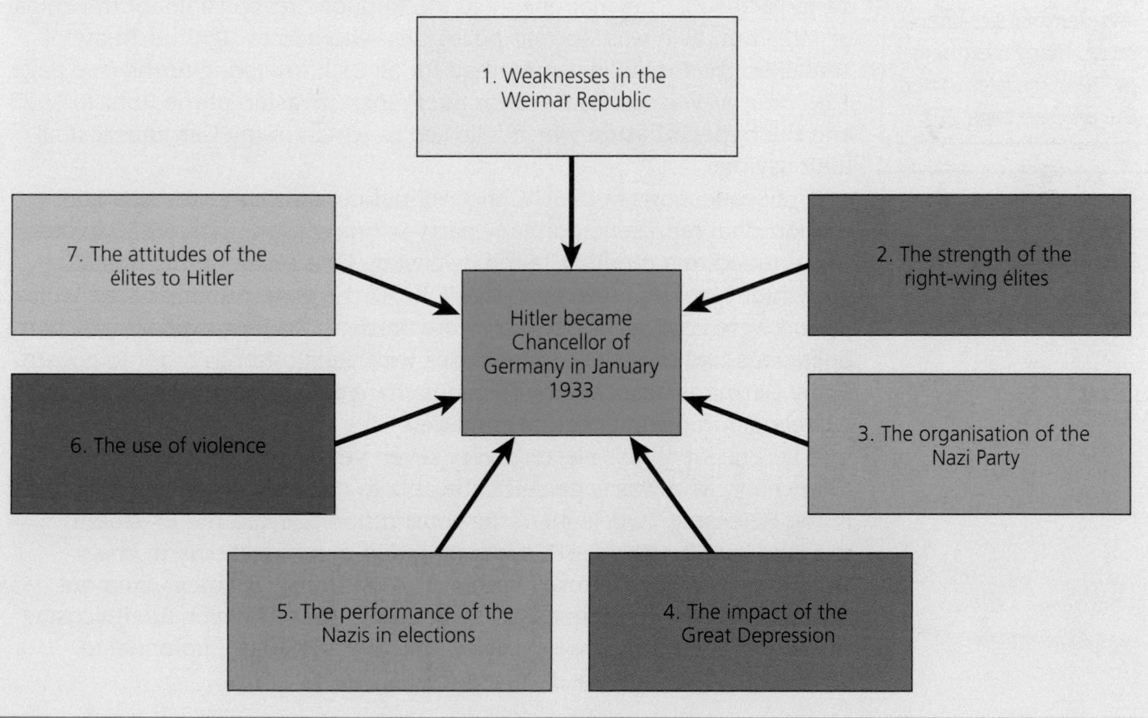

Factor 1: Weaknesses in the Weimar Republic

The Weimar Republic had a liberal constitution, one of the most egalitarian in the world. There were guarantees of freedom of speech, freedom of religion, freedom of the press. All men and women had the right to vote in elections on an equal basis. And yet, throughout the years 1918 to 1933, many Germans could not bring themselves to support the Republic. In this deeply divided nation, democracy had shallow roots.

We have seen that, as Germany faced certain defeat in 1918, the generals ensured that it was not them who got the blame and had to pick up the pieces, but democratic politicians. The Kaiser abdicated on 9 November 1918 amid mutiny and revolution across Germany. The new President, Friedrich Ebert, the leader of the Social Democratic Party, saw his first duty as bringing order and stability to Germany. He had to call on the right-wing paramilitaries of the **Freikorps** to crush the Spartacist (Communist) revolution. Many Communists, including their leaders, were brutally killed. Although defeated, the Communists remained strong and implacably hostile to Weimar democracy in general and the Social Democrats in particular.

Ex-soldiers returning from the war often joined para-military organisations called **Freikorps**. Their views were nationalistic, anti-communist, anti-democratic, often racist. Many members of Freikorps later joined the SA (see page 20)

For more on the significance of the **hyperinflation**, see page 16.

On the other hand, many Germans on the right (see the margin box on page 10) had no real commitment to democracy either (also see page 24 in Factor 2). They not only held the Republic responsible for the defeat of 1918 but, as it was Weimar politicians who had to sign the Treaty of Versailles, the Republic was blamed for all its humiliating terms (see page 13). Weimar was also blamed for the French invasion of the Ruhr in 1923 and the **hyperinflation** which followed in which many Germans lost all their savings.

Unlike elections in the UK, the Weimar constitution was based on proportional representation: any party winning more than 60,000 votes was entitled to a member in the Reichstag. One result of this was the growth of several parties (see page 23). All the governments of the Weimar period were coalitions of two or more parties. Coalitions meant that party politicians had to make compromises with each other in order to govern. Many Germans despised the frequent changes of government and the wheeling and dealing that this involved.

The President was elected every seven years, and appointed the Chancellor, who was expected to be able to command a majority of votes in the Reichstag. Article 48 of the constitution allowed the President to make laws by decree. This was intended to be used only in crisis situations, but Ebert himself used it no less than 135 times – and not always in crises, sometimes just to get a law passed which the Reichstag would not agree to. As we shall see, this Article had the potential to seriously undermine the democratic process.

	Left wing		Centre					Right wing
Initials	KPD	SPD	DDP	Z	BVP	DVP	DNVP	NSDAP
Short name	Communists	Socialists					Nationalists	Nazis
Full German name	Kommunistische Partei Deutschlands	Social-demokratische Partei Deutschlands	Deutsche Demokratische Partei	Zentrum	Bayernische Volkspartei	Deutsche Volkspartei	Deutschnationale Volkspartei	National-sozialistische Deutsche Arbeiterpartei
English name	German Communist Party	Social Democratic Party	German Democratic Party	Centre Party	Bavarian People's Party	German People's Party	German National People's Party	National Socialist German Workers Party
Support from –	Workers and unemployed	Working class, trade unions and socialists	Middle class liberals	Roman Catholics	Bavarians, therefore mainly Roman Catholics	Protestant middle class and industrialists	Industrialists, farmers, independent artisans	(see page 30)
Attitude to Weimar Republic	Hostile – worked for a Communist revolution, like the October 1917 Revolution in Russia	Main creator and supporter of Weimar	Supported	Supported	Supported	Supported	Hostile up to 1925 and in 1933, but support 1925–33	Hostile

△ Main Reichstag parties in the Weimar Republic.

The Weimar Republic was founded in chaos and defeat. However, after 1923 economic stability, even prosperity, brought something like acceptance of the Weimar system. Gustav Zan, leader of the small DVP, was a member of every coalition from 1923 to 1929. Although he hated Versailles as much as anyone, he was a realist, prepared to work within the Weimar constitution. In the 1928 elections, parties hostile to Weimar democracy only received 13 per cent of the votes.

■ Leaving the Nazis out for now, look at the people who supported the other seven parties. What factors brought the voters for each of these parties together: Class? Religion? Region?

■ It is time to weigh up Factor 1 in Hitler's rise to power.

1. Summarise briefly HOW weaknesses in the Weimar Republic may have contributed to Hitler becoming Chancellor.
2. Decide HOW FAR Hitler was responsible for either creating or exploiting this factor.
3. Annotate your causation map by placing the number 1 – near to the central box if you think this was very largely 'his own efforts', further away if you judge that the factor owed little or nothing to his own efforts (or was not down to him at all).
4. Add a sentence to your notes to justify where you have placed Factor 1.

... And be prepared to amend your decision as you learn more about other factors!

Factor 2: The strength of the right-wing élites

In the Kaiser's Germany only certain groups wielded power: aristocrats, big landowners (particularly from Prussia – see map on page 14), army officers, leaders of both Protestant and Roman Catholic Churches, judges and senior civil servants. These were the élites, the people of high status. They believed in hierarchy and order and in monarchy. They were contemptuous of democracy (because it made every voter equal) and loathed socialism (because of its belief in equality and internationalism). Their influence ran strongly through the rest of society. Anyone who had served in the army was guaranteed a government job when they left. The police, post office and civil service were therefore heavily staffed by ex-soldiers, and army attitudes prevailed.

In 1918 the Kaiser and some princes fled, but all the rest of the élites remained in place. Their presence can be seen, for example, in the attitudes of the courts to protest groups. While left-wing groups were savagely sentenced, judges let right-wing groups off lightly. Hitler was tried for attempting to seize power in the 'Beer Hall Putsch' of November 1923, a treasonable offence in which four people died. He was allowed to harangue the court with his views for hours and received only a five-year sentence, of which he served barely more than a year, in considerable comfort.

Further evidence of the continuing strength of the right-wing élites was the success of Hindenburg in the 1925 Presidential election. Already 78 years old, Hindenburg was a symbol of old Prussian militarism. He had fought in the war of 1866, been Supreme Commander of the German Army from 1916–18, and liked to wear his Field Marshal's uniform whenever possible. The old Imperial black, red and white flag was re-introduced for foreign embassies and in the Navy; he made it clear that he did not like working with the Social Democrats.

A number of key words and phrases were regularly used by right-wing newspapers, politicians, writers and preachers, which reveal their nationalist, anti-democratic, often racist views:

- *Volkstum*. The supposed characteristics of the German people: hard-working, upright, sober, creative. There was a racial aspect to this: that all Germans were of the same 'blood'.
- *Űberfremdung*. 'Excessive numbers' of non-Germans were 'flooding' into the country. This usually meant Jews, but also Poles and Slavs, who it was believed were all getting rich at the expense of 'true' Germans, and weakening their racial purity.
- *Dolchstoss*. The 'stab in the back' which brought defeat to the heroic German Army in 1918.
- *Schmährepublik*. A shameful joke republic – Weimar.
- *Drittes Reich*. What Germany needed was a Third Empire (after the first, the medieval Holy Roman Empire, and the Second Empire of 1871–1918).
- *Führer*. A leader who understood all that was German, who would lead the German people out of their humiliation.
- *Kampf*. The struggle which would be necessary to make their country great again.

■ Now decide what you think about Factor 2: the strength of the right-wing élites.

For this factor, apply the same instructions as those we gave on page 23 when you thought about Factor 1.

Factor 3: Nazi Party organisation

As he sat in the Landsberg prison in 1924, Hitler had plenty of time to decide what to do next. It seemed that he could not seize power through violence: he would therefore have to win it through the democratic electoral system which he despised. 'We must hold our noses and enter the Reichstag,' he told his followers. The speeches he had made at his trial had made him nationally known, but the Nazi Party was a small Munich-based party and he was banned from speaking in public until 1927.

Hitler spent the next five years building the Nazi Party into a national movement. In each Reichstag constituency a local Nazi Party was set up, under a trusted Nazi leader – a *gauleiter*. There were also national Nazi organisations for different groups: farmers, teachers, students and so on. Members were expected to carry out door-to-door leafleting, but were kept involved through regular meetings and rallies. Marches, with massed flags, bands and uniformed SA (see page 20) with swastika banners brought the Nazis to the attention of every German in every town. Speakers had to carry out a year-long monthly training course, then make at least 30 speeches in 8 months before becoming an official party speaker.

The Nazis claimed to be not just a party, but a 'movement'. It ran soup-kitchens for families in financial difficulties and provided hostels for rootless young SA recruits. In this way, it set out to demonstrate the *Völksgemeinschaft*, or People's Community, all pulling together, which Hitler called for in his speeches (see Enquiry 5, page 52).

As the Nazi 'movement' grew, Hitler sometimes had to fight to keep control of it. A more left-wing trend emerged, emphasising hostility to banks and big business and led by Gregor Strasser in northern and western Germany. Although the Nazi Party had the word 'Socialist' in its name, Hitler was no socialist. When he spoke about 'the workers', he meant 'workers by mind and hand', that is, all Germans, which led straight to his racial ideas about **Aryan** superiority. At a meeting in Bamberg in 1926, Hitler faced his rivals down. From then on, a key feature of Nazi propaganda was the *Führerprinzip* – the need for a strong leader, Hitler. The greeting 'Heil Hitler' and the Nazi salute became compulsory.

Organising the Nazi Party and running the welfare system were expensive. Most of the money came from membership fees and donations collected at meetings. Contrary to the views of some Marxist historians who characterised Nazism as a front for bourgeois capitalists, it did not have widespread support among industrialists at this stage, but Hitler was beginning to cultivate some rich supporters. The iron and steel magnate, Fritz Thyssen, and Alfred Hugenberg, owner of several newspapers, liked Hitler's anti-Communist stance and gave money to the Party.

The term '**Aryan**', which is of Sanskrit origin, was used by nineteenth century 'race scientists' to describe speakers of Indo-European languages. These included Romans, Czechs, Celts, Iranians, Slavs and western Europeans. Nazi racists defined 'Aryan' more narrowly, as north-west Europeans, and claimed they were a superior race.

△ A Nazi poster from 1932. It says: 'Workers of the mind and hand! Vote for the front soldier Hitler!'

■ Now decide what you think about Factor 3: the organisation of the Nazi Party.

Once again, apply the same instructions as those we gave on page 23 when you thought about Factor 1.

Gradually the Nazi Party gained support. From 27,000 members in 1924 it had grown to 100,000 by the end of 1928. By then it had mopped up most of the other little extremist right-wing parties. Other key Nazis joined at this time, including Göbbels, Himmler and Bormann (see pages 34–35). It had a national organisation and, although it was not truly all-class and all-region, at least it was widely known.

Yet in the elections of May 1928 it only received 2.6 per cent of the votes, giving the Nazis just twelve members in the Reichstag, two less than in 1924.

Factor 4: The impact of the Great Depression

Crash and Depression

Gustav **Stresemann** (1878–1929), was an important member of every government in Germany from 1923 to 1929. Although a nationalist who hated the terms of the Treaty of Versailles, he believed that Germany's best interests were served by negotiating better relations with other countries.

For a few years in the second half of the 1920s Germany experienced some brief economic growth. This was largely due to loans from the USA under the Dawes Plan, negotiated by **Stresemann** and US Treasury Secretary Charles Dawes in 1924.

However, this recovery was precarious. Interest rates were high and loans mostly short-term. In 1928 the world economy dipped. By early 1929 unemployment, always relatively high in Germany, reached 2.5 million. But far worse was to come. On 24 October 1929 panic hit the New York stock exchange on Wall Street: 16.4 million shares were sold at ever plummeting prices. US banks began to call in their loans, precipitating a run on German investments. Banks began to fail and businesses began to lay off workers. With less money to spend, demand for goods, even food, dwindled. By 1932 18,000 farmers and 50,000 businesses had gone bankrupt.

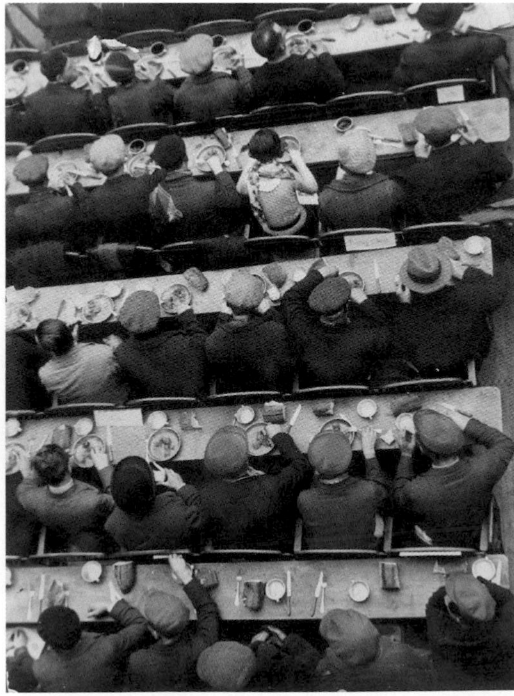

◁ Food for jobless people, Berlin, 1933.

Month by month the situation deteriorated. By 1932, unemployment had reached 6 million, or one-third of all workers. With their dependents, 13 million people were affected – probably more, as many workers were on short-time or reduced wages and many women workers did not register as unemployed. It was not only the working class which suffered; middle class bank workers, civil servants, shopkeepers and those in service occupations such as restaurateurs all suffered too.

The Great Depression was not just an economic catastrophe: it had profound psychological effects. People without work felt useless, their lives wasted. Queuing for the few jobs available or relying on charity for food, as in the photo opposite, was humiliating. As people looked for who to blame, the Weimar government, never widely respected anyway, came in for fierce criticism.

The response of the Weimar governments

Stresemann died just three weeks before the Wall Street Crash and the coalition government he had helped to keep together soon fell apart. The DVP wanted to meet the looming crisis by cutting unemployment benefit; the SPD, the party of trade unions and workers, refused, and Chancellor Müller resigned in March 1930.

From then on Germany became less and less of a democracy. No Chancellor commanded a majority in the Reichstag. President Hindenburg was never a strong supporter of democracy and preferred a more right-wing, authoritarian government. He was prepared to use his powers under Article 48 of the Weimar constitution if the Reichstag would not support him. His natural links were with the old élites in the army, which increased in political importance. The man Hindenburg called on to be the next Chancellor was Friedrich Brüning, an ex-army officer, leader of the Centre Party.

Brüning set out to deal with the increasing economic crisis by making savage cuts to public expenditure. Memories of the disastrous hyperinflation of 1923 meant that deflation was regarded as the only option. Unemployment benefit was cut, and so was the length of time for which it could be claimed. Cuts of one-third were made to pensions to victims of the First World War. As the Great Depression continued and unemployment went on rising, real hardship hit millions of families. Brüning became known as the 'Hunger Chancellor'. When he failed to get Reichstag support for further cuts he called an election for September 1930. The results were startling: the Communists increased their vote to 13 per cent of the electorate; but the Nazis won 18.3 per cent and sent 107 members into the Reichstag.

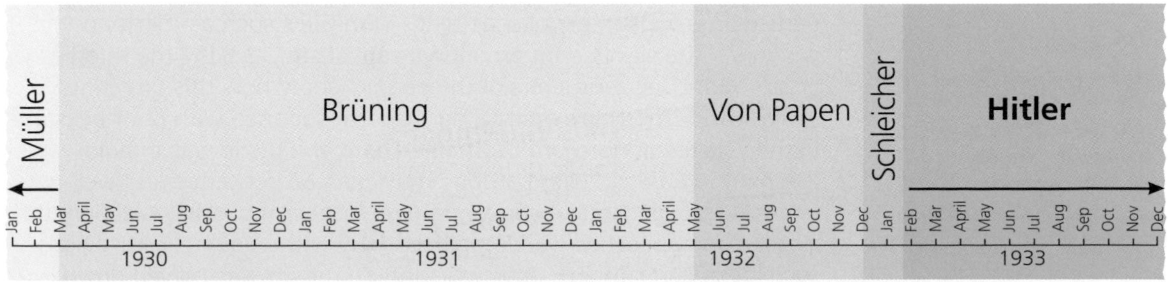

△ Chancellors of Germany January 1930–December 1933. Hitler remained in power until May 1945.

△ Nazi brownshirts parading without their brown shirts – or, in some cases, without shirts at all, following the ban on political uniforms imposed by Chancellor Brüning in 1931.

From then on, with increasing violence on the streets and even in the Reichstag (see Factor 6, page 31), power now passed to Hindenburg and those around him. Brüning had to rely increasingly on Article 48 in order to rule: by late 1932 Germany was hardly a functioning democracy, with Hindenburg's nominees ruling by decree. Brüning increased press censorship and tried to curb the Nazis by banning the wearing of political uniforms. This had little effect on the SA, as the photo opposite shows.

An election for President had to take place in 1932. Hindenburg, now aged 85, hoped to be allowed to continue as President without an election, but could not get the constitution changed. Hitler hurriedly became a German citizen in order to stand. He waged a spectacular campaign, winning 36.8 per cent of the votes.

Brüning was falling out of favour with Hindenburg, who, in May 1932, was persuaded to get rid of him and try someone else. This was Franz **von Papen**, a wealthy landowner, most of whose Cabinet did not even sit in the Reichstag – nicknamed 'the cabinet of barons'. Von Papen called for new elections in July 1932. The parties which had supported Weimar democracy lost support, with the Communists polling 14.5 per cent of the vote; the Nazis, however, increased their share to 37.4 per cent, giving them 230 Reichstag members.

Although he was a member of the Centre Party (like Brüning), **von Papen's** ministers were members of other right-wing parties – or none. They could not command a majority in the Reichstag, but had the support of President Hindenburg. He used his power under Article 48 to enable von Papen to rule by decree.

Factor 5: The performance of the Nazis in elections

The terrible suffering of the German people during the Great Depression provided an opportunity for extremist parties like the Communists and the Nazis. But that alone does not explain the extraordinary rise in support for the Nazis in the elections of 1930 and 1932. The work Hitler had done in the years after his release from prison in 1924 in building the Party, together with Göbbels brilliant propaganda skills, meant the Nazis were ready and able to tap into voters' anxieties, bringing them great success. There were several aspects to this.

1 **Targeted appeal.** The structure of the Party, with local and special interest groups, meant that they could target the grievances of particular groups of people. Meetings with titles such as 'German workers – the slaves of international capitalism', 'Saving the middle class', 'Marxists: murderers of the people' show how this targeting could work'. The Nazis found a particular resonance with poor peasants in the villages of northern Germany. There, the tactic was to hold 'German Evenings', with patriotic music, an SA presence and well-known local speakers to concentrate on local complaints. Anti-Semitic slogans and speeches were employed only with audiences for whom such ideas had support; otherwise anti-Semitism was played down.

■ Now decide what you think about Factor 4: the impact of the Great Depression.

Once again, apply the same instructions as those we gave on page 23 when you thought about Factor 1.

2 **Dynamic image.** Nazi Party membership grew from 100,000 in 1928 to 300,000 by 1930 and nearly 800,000 by 1932. Members were kept frantically busy, especially during elections. Frequent meetings, rallies, processions and mass leafleting meant that every German was made aware of the Nazis. Striking posters met their eyes on every street. Göbbels sent out a regular flurry of new campaigns and new slogans.

The image generated by all this activity was that the Nazis were a modern, dynamic, orderly and disciplined 'movement'. Hitler was the first to use an aeroplane to visit every major town and city during the 1932 presidential election campaign. The marches, with brass bands, flags and ranks of uniformed SA appealed to a nation with a strong military tradition. They gave the impression that the Nazis represented order and purpose, in contrast to what seemed like the endless and futile debates of the Reichstag politicians. (See, for example, the cartoon on this page.)

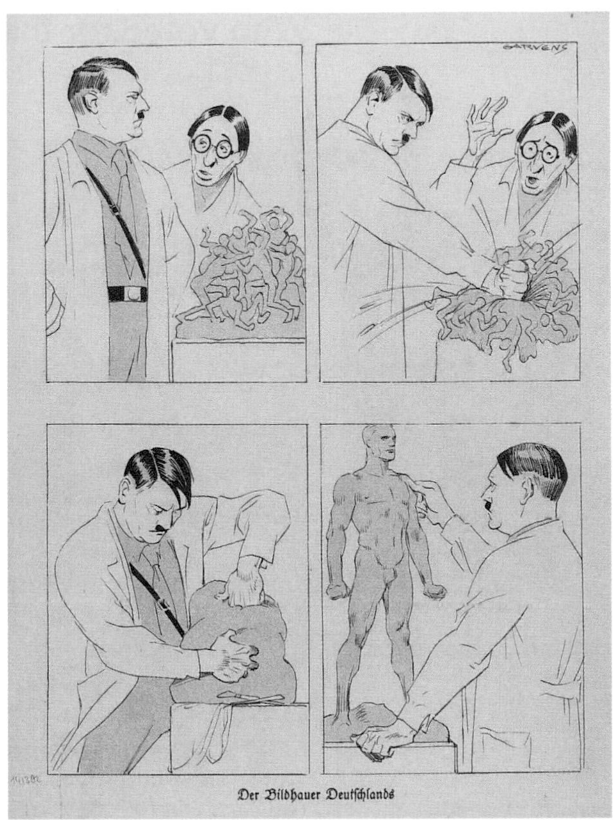

△ **A Nazi cartoon from 1932 called 'Germany's Sculptor'. Think about the range of messages being conveyed here.**

3 **The programme.** Nazi speakers did not present a detailed programme. They made attractive promises: to deal with mass unemployment and get everyone back to work; to make Germany great again; to crush the menace of Communism. They presented themselves as a patriotic third way, different from the Marxist revolutionaries on the left and the capitalists' failed policy of deflation on the right. Their view was that Germany would solve its own problems when the German people rose up and worked together with a common purpose. **Autarky**, the Nazi plan to make Germany self-sufficient, had obvious nationalist appeal.

For the **autarky** policies in practice, see page 91.

4 **The leader.** Hitler was able to use his remarkable oratorical skills to new mass audiences. During the 1932 presidential campaign he made 46 speeches. The appeal of the leader, rising up from the people to show them the way out of their distress to harmony and well-being, the *Führerprinzip*, was deep-rooted in Germany.

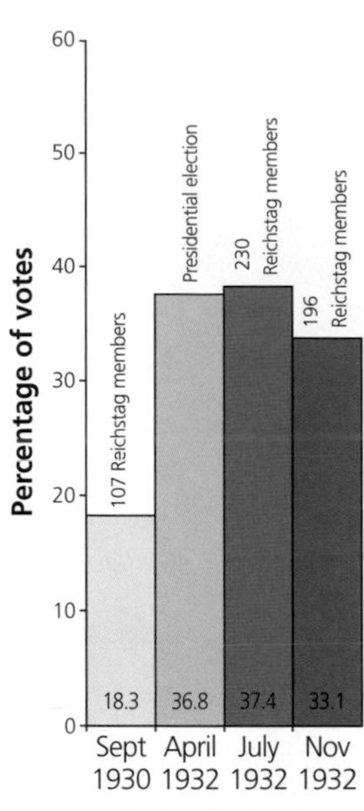

△ Nazi Election results.

Who voted for the Nazis?

The results of the September 1930 election show the changes that had taken place in voters' allegiances for the main parties since the 1928 election.

PARTY	No. of seats before election	No. of seats after election	Gains (+) or losses (–)
Centre (the party of Chancellor, Brüning, who had called the election)	63	68	+5
Social Democrats – SPD	153	143	–10
Nationalists – DNVP	73	41	–32
People's Party – DVP	45	31	–13
Communists – KPD	54	77	+23
Nazis – NSDAP	12	107	+95

Not surprisingly most of those who voted for the Nazis seem to have come from the more right-wing, Nationalist and People's Parties, but they also seem to have stolen some support from the Social Democrats.

For many years up to the 1990s Marxists and historians of the left portrayed the Nazis as primarily a party of the middle, rather than working classes. These were people who were worried about law and order, protecting their property and dealing with the threat of Communism. The Nazis certainly promised all these things, and certainly working class Germans did not give overwhelming support for the Nazis. Nazi support in the big working class cities and areas like Berlin, Hamburg and the Ruhr was always less than other areas. But was it all so clear-cut?

Two things have changed historians' analyses of Nazi supporters.

1 First, with the fall of the Berlin Wall and German unification in 1991, archives kept secret in the former East Germany have been opened up.
2 Secondly, computers have made possible the analysis of large amounts of data.

Current analyses of some class/occupation groups and their support for the Nazis in 1932 now look more like this:

Class	% of the population	% of Nazi support
Working class	46	31
White-collar workers – lower middle class	12	21
Self-employed	10	18
Civil servants (includes teachers, postal workers, police, etc.)	5	7
Peasants and small farmers	21	12

The earlier analysis, that the Nazis gained their support disproportionately from the lower middle class, self-employed and civil servants, still stands. Also that they never had widespread working class support seems to hold true – but not that true. Workers made up nearly half the population of Germany, and nearly a third of Nazi votes came from workers. Current research is trying to break down the details here: a worker is not just a worker; he or she may be a Protestant or a Roman Catholic, work in a huge factory, or a tiny craft workshop, belong to a trade union, or not.

Other trends seem to be becoming clear:

- Religion: the Nazis did twice as well among Protestants as Roman Catholics.
- Region: These religious allegiances brought them more support in the north than in the strongly Roman Catholic areas of the south and the west.
- Trade unions: The Nazis did better among workers in small, independent, non-unionised workplaces than among trade union members.
- Gender: Women (at least those who were not Roman Catholic) voted disproportionately for the Nazis.
- Age: Nazi voters were older than the average voter.

We could conclude that people who had strong links to other communities, such as the Roman Catholic Church, or trade unions, tended not to support the Nazis. But more research into specific towns, trades and communities may produce more subtle conclusions.

■ Now decide what you think about Factor 5: the performance of the Nazis in elections.

As before, apply the same instructions as those given on page 23 when you thought about Factor 1.

Factor 6: Violence

Violence was endemic throughout the Weimar period. Both left- and right-wing groups led uprisings which brought armed men onto the streets in 1919 and 1920. Political assassinations took place throughout the 1920s. The Nazi Party set up the SA as early as 1921 to 'protect' their speakers, but also to break up rival meetings. Other organisations had their uniformed fighters too: the 'Red Front' of the Communists and the 'Reichsbanner' of the SPD. These were not petty scraps: clubs, brass knuckle-dusters, heavy buckled belts and chair-legs were commonly used. The Nazis claimed that 29 of their members had been killed between 1924 and 1929 and the Red Front and Reichsbanner claimed similar numbers. Violence increased during the Depression years and especially during elections. The Communists said they had suffered 44 deaths in fights with the Nazis in 1930 and the Reichsbanner over 50. Police reported 82 deaths in the seven weeks leading up to the July 1932 election.

Hitler did not hide his support for violence. His speeches were full of violent language, like 'smash', 'crush', 'attack', 'destroy'; his gestures were violent. He insisted that violent struggle was inevitable and that war was the highest activity humans could aspire to. In *Mein Kampf* he described his Stormtroopers in action at an early meeting in a Munich beer hall:

> The trouble had not begun when my storm-troopers attacked. Like wolves, they flung themselves in packs of eight or ten upon the enemy. I hardly saw one of them who was not covered in blood. The hall looked almost as if a shell had struck it. Many of my supporters were being bandaged, others had to be driven away, but we remained masters of the situation.

It is arguable whether their brawling did the Nazis any good. It heightened the atmosphere of crisis in the years 1932–33, of things getting out of control, emphasising the need for order and tough discipline – which the Nazis claimed to offer. The violence of the SA certainly encouraged a certain type of person to join them. Ernst Röhm, leader of the SA, built up the numbers of the SA to 60,000 by 1930, 400,000 by 1933. He explained his own reasons for being in the SA:

> Since I am an immature and wicked person, war and unrest appeal to me more than well-behaved bourgeois order.

■ Now decide what you think about Factor 6: the performance of the Nazis in elections.
Once again, apply the same instructions as those given on page 23 for Factor 1.

To some, the sight of Nazis beating up Communists was welcome. However, to others, this street-fighting image was distasteful, and, as we shall see, was a reason why some people who agreed with many Nazi policies did not support them.

Factor 7: The attitudes of the élites to Hitler

By the middle of 1932 democracy in Germany was long gone. Elections were held, but decisions about who should wield power rested with Hindenburg and those around him, the old élites. In a properly-functioning democracy, Hitler, as the leader of the largest party in the Reichstag following the Nazis' spectacular success in the July 1932 elections, should have been asked to become Chancellor. But Hindenburg wouldn't appoint him. Although they shared many of the same views, on the German nation, the Treaty of Versailles, the need for authoritarian rule and so on, a vast gulf of class and status divided them. To Hindenburg the Nazis were vulgar, uneducated street-fighters, led by a former corporal.

For the next six months the increasingly senile Hindenburg and his élite associates dithered between two alternatives:

A Send the Reichstag packing and hand power over to the army. Many in the army were eager for this to happen, but the élites feared a civil war would be the result.

B Find some way of bringing Hitler into the government, using his support in the Reichstag to pass laws, while keeping him under control.

Chancellor von Papen favoured Option A, but had a massive vote of no confidence against him in the Reichstag and was forced to call new elections for November. The election result produced a crisis for the Nazis.

They polled 2 million fewer votes than in July, cutting their Reichstag members to 196, although they were still the largest party. The parties of the left, the SPD, with 131 seats and the Communists with 100, could have out-voted them, but they had been hostile to each other for too long to work together.

There were fierce arguments in the Nazi Party about what to do next: should they join with another party in a coalition, even if Hitler was not Chancellor, and so get a taste of power? The German electorate seemed quite volatile: was a vote for them any more than a protest vote, which could drift away as quickly as it came? Also, frequent elections had left the Party almost bankrupt. Another alternative was to seize power by force, as many of Röhm's 800,000 Stormtroopers wanted to. Hitler kept his nerve and held out for the Chancellorship.

By December 1932 von Papen had lost the support of Hindenburg, who appointed General **Schleicher** as Chancellor. Von Papen now intrigued with Hindenburg against Schleicher and turned to Option B: give Hitler what he wanted, the position of Chancellor, but give the Nazis only two other cabinet posts and pack the rest of the cabinet with reliable right-wing non-Nazis, including von Papen himself as Vice Chancellor. That way, the old élites would stay in power, with Hitler as their puppet, delivering Nazi votes in the Reichstag. Hindenburg agreed, and Hitler was appointed.

'We have hired him,' von Papen was heard to say.

Kurt **Schleicher**, 1882–1934 was a German Army general of extreme right-wing views, who was close to Hindenburg.

Now decide what you think about Factor 7: the attitudes of the élites to Hitler.

Once again, apply the same instructions as those given on page 23 for Factor 1.

Concluding your Enquiry

1. Look again at your final diagram and the sentences you've written summarising the factors and how far you judge they support the view that Hitler became Chancellor through his own efforts. You may already have made changes as you have worked through the enquiry, but do you want to change anything else now?
2. Now for the next stage. Are there any links between the different factors? Draw lines across your diagram, linking any factors which are connected in some way. Write what the connection is on the line you drew.
3. Does your diagram – including these links – support the view that Hitler became Chancellor mainly through his own efforts? If there are several factors very close to the central box then that suggests he was mainly responsible for his appointment 'through his own efforts'.
4. British historian Ian Kershaw seems to think the opposite – that Hitler's own efforts weren't mainly responsible for Hitler becoming Chancellor. He wrote, in 1991: 'By January 1933, with all other options apparently exhausted, most [of the élite groups], with the big landowners well to the fore, were prepared to entertain a Hitler government. Had they opposed it, a Hitler Chancellorship would have been inconceivable. Hitler needed the élite to attain power. But by January 1933, they in turn needed Hitler as he alone could deliver the mass support required to impose a tenable authoritarian solution to Germany's crisis of capitalism and crisis of the state.'

   Do you agree with Kershaw? If there are several factors that Hitler's efforts did little or nothing to exploit, then he cannot be said to have become Chancellor through his own efforts.
5. Finally, write up your own conclusion using the evidence summarised on your diagram.

Hitler's right-hand men

◁ Hitler and leading Nazis at a meeting of the National Socialist Women's League in Nuremberg in 1935. The woman beside Hitler is Gertrud Scholtz-Klink, who, as head of this League, was the most senior woman in the Nazi state – but even she had no say in political decision-making.

Hitler did not gain power without help, and once he was in power, even as dictator, he did not rule alone. To give you some idea of the nature of the leading Nazis who helped shape Germany from 1933 to 1945, here are brief outlines of the top-ranking Nazis who happen to be sitting alongside their leader in this image. Starting with the person sitting to Hitler's right they are: Rudolf Hess, Heinrich Himmler, Wilhelm Frick, Josef Göbbels and Martin Bormann.

Rudolf Hess fought in the trenches in the First World War before studying Geopolitics at Munich University. He joined the new German Workers' Party (DAP) and met Hitler, quickly becoming one of Hitler's closest and most trusted friends. Like Hitler, he was a non-smoking, non-drinking vegetarian. He was also a keen mountain walker, pilot and astrologist with a belief in the occult. When the 1923 Munich Putsch failed (see page 19), Hess was imprisoned with Hitler in Landsberg where he edited *Mein Kampf* after Hitler had dictated it to him. In 1933 he became deputy party leader and, in effect, deputy Führer, but he offered little more than blind faith in Hitler's leadership. As Hitler became preoccupied with war after 1939, Hess lost confidence in him. In 1941 he flew to Scotland hoping to negotiate peace with the British government but was arrested and held in Britain for the rest of the war. At the Nuremberg Trials in 1945–46, Hess was sentenced to life imprisonment rather than death as he was not found guilty of crimes against humanity. He spent the rest of his life in Spandau prison in Berlin where, in 1987, he was discovered with an electrical cord around his neck, suggesting he committed suicide.

Heinrich Himmler was an ex-chicken farmer who became head of the SS. In 1929 this was a small section within the SA, with fewer than 300 members but Himmler built it up to 52,000 by 1934. He proved unreservedly loyal to Hitler. In 1939 Hitler agreed to let him merge the SS intelligence service and the Gestapo (the Secret Police) with the Criminal Police, giving Himmler one of the most powerful roles in the Nazi regime. Historians have called his SS 'a state within a state'. The Death's Head Units of the SS, led by Himmler and Reinhard Heydrich, had the specific job of killing Jews and other victims of Nazism (see Chapter 8). In May 1945, Himmler was captured by British troops but committed suicide before his trial. He had a strong belief in astrology, the occult and reincarnation: he believed that in an earlier life he had been a medieval German king.

Wilhelm Frick was a lawyer in Bavaria in the early 1920s. He supported Hitler's Munich Putsch in 1923. In 1924 he was elected to the Reichstag for a small right-wing party and joined the Nazis in 1925, serving as Hitler's Minister of the Interior from 1933 to 1943. He helped shape the anti-Jewish Nuremberg Laws but his power declined from 1936 onwards as Himmler took over most of his responsibilities. He was found guilty of crimes against humanity after the war and was hanged in 1946.

Josef Göbbels grew to be only 5 feet tall due to a condition he suffered when he was a toddler that meant his right leg was permanently twisted. He had an inferiority complex about his physical appearance despite being one of the few Nazis with a university education, having gained a Ph.D. from the University of Heidelberg. He created the Nazi newspaper *Der Angriff* in 1927 and was soon put in charge of Party propaganda. As Minister for Public Enlightenment Göbbels was indispensable to Hitler in projecting the Nazi message through radio, films, posters and the 1936 Olympic Games, using methods that were ahead of their time. He encouraged the burning of left-wing and Jewish books which he labelled 'un-German'. He was a skilful orator and, although distrusted by other leading Nazis, he remained loyal to Hitler to the end. On 1 May 1945, the day after Hitler's death, Göbbels poisoned his own children and shot his wife before committing suicide.

Martin Bormann was the son of a post office worker. He dropped out of school with little formal education. He served briefly in the army during the Great War and then joined the Freikorps during which time he was sent to prison for being an accessory to murder. On his release, Bormann joined the Nazi Party and became its business manager and Chief of Staff to Rudolf Hess. When Hess flew to Scotland in 1941 Bormann was promoted. As a way of securing favour, he gave Hitler a dog that became one of his favourite pets. Bormann built up a huge power base within the Nazi regime, first by overseeing contributions to the Party from rich businessmen and then by overseeing Hitler's personal finances. He exercised enormous power as he could control who had access to the Führer. At the end of the war he disappeared amid rumours that he had committed suicide. In 1972, a skeleton was uncovered buried underground in Berlin and later tests identified it as Bormann.

4 What led to Germany's descent into dictatorship?

When Adolf Hitler was sworn in as Chancellor on 31 January 1933, Germany was still officially a democracy. By 2 August 1934 it was not. In their first eighteen months in power, the Nazis transformed the democratic Weimar Republic into the dictatorial Third Reich. The change was swift but the fact that it happened should have surprised no one. Hitler had been clear about his intentions for years. Here, for example, is part of a speech he delivered in the campaign leading up to the July 1932 election:

> Our opponents accuse us National Socialists, and me in particular, of being intolerant and quarrelsome. They say that we don't want to work with other parties. They say the National Socialists are not German at all, because they refuse to work with other political parties. So is it typically German to have thirty parties? ... These gentlemen are quite right. We are intolerant. I have given myself one goal – to sweep these thirty political parties out of Germany. They mistake us for one of them. We have one aim, and we will follow it fanatically and ruthlessly to the grave.

△ The leaders of the Nazi Party, taken on the day Hitler became Chancellor. Standing, left to right: Kube, Kerrl, Göbbels, Hitler, Röhm, Göring, Darre, Himmler, Hess. Seated: Frick.

You have read about Göbbels, Himmler, Hess and Frick on pages 34–35.

Wilhelm Kube worked to Nazify the Protestant Church. During the war he infamously threw sweets to Jewish children as they were being buried alive.

Hans Kerrl, like Kube, worked to Nazify the Church, but gradually faded from power.

Ernst Röhm was the brutal, hard-drinking leader of the SA. For reasons you will soon learn, his face was removed from later versions of this image.

Hermann Göring was a powerful figure, for many years second only to Hitler. A glamorous fighter pilot in the 1914–18 war, he was so vain that he would change his clothes up to five times a day.

Walther Darre became Minister for Agriculture, applying theories of selective breeding not only to farmstock but to humans.

Enquiry Focus: What led to Germany's descent into dictatorship?

Hitler had made no secret of his desire for a one party state in Germany and, when it happened, he insisted that the change was enacted legally bit by bit. The diagram below shows on each step, a decree or law that took Germany further down its descent to dictatorship.

It may seem that the diagram alone answers the enquiry question – it was these laws, passed by Hitler's government, that led Germany to become a one party state under one man's rule. But there is much more to it than that. Good history never stops with the story, the narrative. It involves analysis as well. It asks what happened and why. Was everything as it appeared to be?

As you work through this enquiry, you will learn about these events and about the shifting events and developments that lay beneath each law. At intervals, you will be prompted to do three things:

1. Make notes about the events and the underlying developments that we explain in each section. This will give you a clear grasp of the facts and the main issues you need to understand.
2. Decide for yourself whether or not the events in that section suggest Hitler was working within the law.
3. Decide, in each section, whether the decree or act deserves to be given pride of place on the step. Maybe one of the underlying events did more to determine Germany's descent into dictatorship than the decree or act we have shown. You will have to make up your mind and justify your conclusion.

At the end of the enquiry you will design your own diagram based on your analysis of the most significant moments in deciding Germany's fate between January 1933 and August 1934.

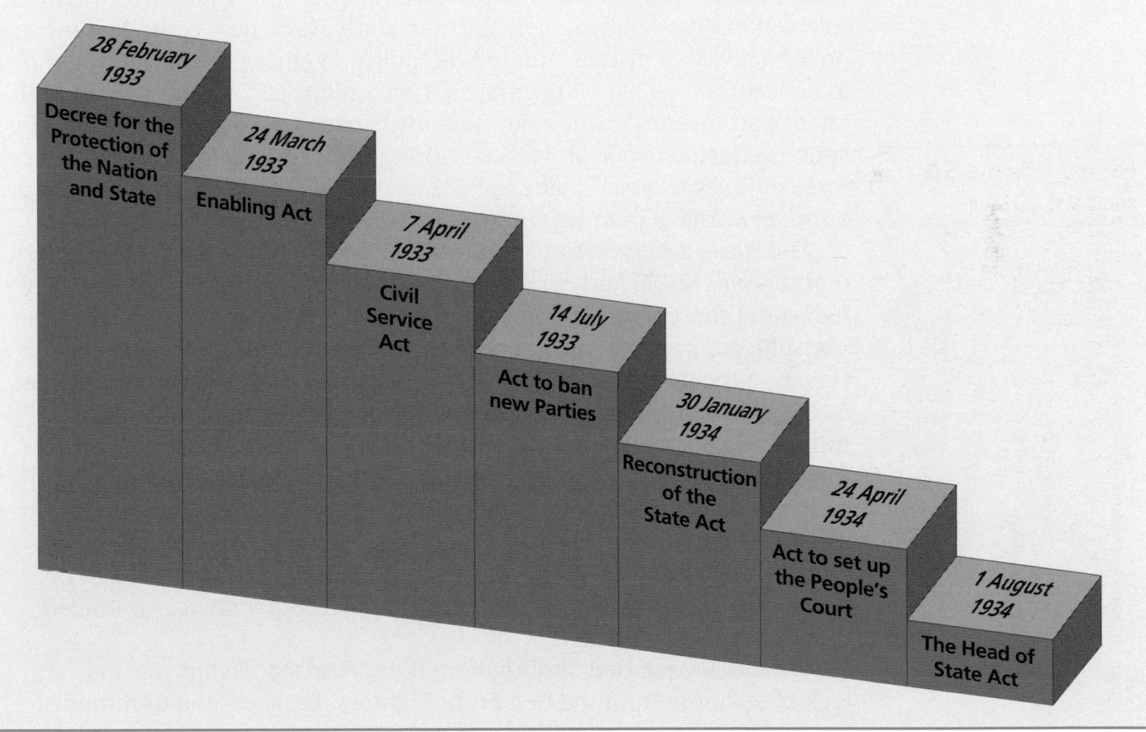

Step 1: The Decree for the Protection of the Nation and State – 28 February 1933

Persuasion and coercion

On 1 February, two days after Hitler became Chancellor, President Hindenburg dissolved the Reichstag and called an election for 5 March. The calling of these elections had been one of Hitler's conditions for becoming Chancellor. The coalition cabinet was full of right-wing politicians but included only **three Nazis**. Hitler believed the elections would give him a majority in the Reichstag so that he could rule without a coalition, fill his cabinet with Nazis and pass any legislation he wanted.

The **three Nazis** in the cabinet were Hitler, Göring and Frick. The remaining nine seats went to members of other right-wing parties, notably von Papen who, as Deputy Chancellor naïvely believed he could control Hitler.

Persuading the electorate to vote for the Nazis was made easier as the Party could now use the state's resources to supplement its own. Swastika flags flew prominently and the state radio service broadcast Hitler's speeches. Businessmen and most Germans with something to lose feared a Communist government more than anything else and Hitler made the destruction of Marxism his only real promise of the campaign, remaining vague on all details. Large businesses poured funds into the Nazi Party, now that it was in a position of power.

But persuasion was not the only method used by the Nazis. With Frick as the Reich's Ministry of the Interior and Göring holding the same role within Prussia, the largest German state, Nazis now controlled most police activity. They duly ordered the police to ignore Nazi activities and to concentrate on left-wing groups. Trade unionists, Communists and SPD rallies and meetings were now violently broken up by the **SA** without any serious effort at police protection. Göring even created an auxiliary police force in Prussia largely made up of SA brownshirts who could then carry out their criminal intimidation with some doubtful claim to legitimacy.

For more on the **SA** see page 20.

The Nazis also tried to ban SPD newspapers. When the SPD claimed that this was illegal and challenged the government's ban in courts, they had some success, but time had passed, the SPD's public voice had been silenced and its image as an enemy of the people had been spread. However, the parties on the left continued to be their own worst enemies as the SPD and Communists refused to co-operate, perpetuating the mutual hatred that started when the SPD Weimar government crushed the Communist risings in 1918 and 1919. So, while the SPD fought in the courts, the SA set about threatening or using physical violence to silence the Nazis' political enemies on the streets. At times Hitler insisted that he did not approve of SA brutality, claiming that the incidents must be the work of people trying to discredit his party. But violence continued unchecked.

What really puzzled and frightened the Nazi leadership was the lack of response from the Red Front Fighters' League – the Communist paramilitary. The Communists may have believed Hitler's appointment was the last desperate act of the capitalist system to save itself and that in time a Marxist revolution was sure to succeed, or they may simply have feared the army that backed Hitler. Whatever the reason, they lay low. Hitler was convinced that they were planning a massive uprising to take place at any time. And then came the event that allowed him to take the initiative.

Fire and fury

△ **The Reichstag building on fire on 27 February, 1933.**

On the night of 27 February the people of Berlin were shocked to see smoke and flames emerging from the Reichstag. This building was the architectural symbol, not only of German democracy, but also of the pre-Weimar German government, and it was ablaze. By the next morning, the building's interior had been destroyed, gutted by the fire, while the outer shell continued to smoke as the Berlin fire brigade could only douse the smouldering building with water.

It was soon announced that the fire had been started by Marinus van der Lubbe, an unemployed Dutch labourer and member of the Communist youth movement. He had broken in and had started fires, first in a restaurant, then in the debating chamber and then through the rest of the building before being caught by Reichstag officials. At this news, shock turned to fury in Berlin.

Speaking with the Nazi leadership the next day Hitler dismissed the emerging evidence that van der Lubbe had acted alone. Within hours the police began rounding up all known Communists across the country. Over 4000 were taken, including over 100 Reichstag deputies and thousands of other elected Communist officials.

The Decree

Even before the Reichstag fire, the full coalition cabinet had already considered a proposal that Hindenberg should issue an emergency Presidential Decree for the protection of the Nation and State to legitimise a wave of arrests and imprisonment without trial, just like the one unleashed on 28 February. It proposed severe restrictions on freedom of speech and freedom of assembly. The coalition now voted through these same measures with an extra provision that gave the cabinet, rather than the President, the power to take over public order in any federated state if there was a threat to public order.

On 28 February, President Hindenburg signed this emergency decree, giving a fearsome array of emergency powers to a cabinet that very soon, after the March elections, was to be dominated by Hitler and the Nazis.

■ Now do the three tasks described on page 37 for this decree:

1. Make your notes.
2. Decide whether Hitler was acting legally.
3. Decide whether the Decree should be replaced on the top of this step by some other event or development that did more to cause Germany's descent to dictatorship. Justify your decision.

Step 2: The Enabling Act – 24 March 1933

The election

The final days of the election campaign leading to the vote on 5 March 1933 were conducted in an atmosphere of fear and intimidation. Hindenburg's Decree for the Protection of the Nation and the State gave the government wide-ranging powers to search private homes, arrest individuals, and check people's mail. The state, often working through the SA in its role as an auxiliary police force, used these new powers to seize and assault socialists and any Communists not yet arrested after the Reichstag fire. This made it virtually impossible for them to run conventional campaigns. At the same time the Nazi electoral machine was seemingly unstoppable. Göbbels exploited the shock of the fire and raised the spectre of a Communist revolution. Nazi newspapers printed vicious anti-Communist stories blaming them for the Reichstag fire and accusing them of being traitors who were in league with the Communists in Russia.

The Nazis were relying on these methods to neutralise their main opposition and win a majority in the Reichstag. If the Social Democrat and Communist electoral machines could not function effectively, their core voters would perhaps stay away on voting day. But, at this stage, Hitler decided against going as far as banning the Communist party, fearing that this might simply transfer more votes to the SPD. It suited the Nazis that their left-wing rivals should remain divided.

But for all their advantages, when the election was over, the results were surprising. Hitler had failed to win the outright majority he so desperately wanted.

PARTY	Reichstag seats before the election	Reichstag seats after the election	Gains or Losses
Centre Party – Z	70	74	+4
Social Democrat Party – SDP	121	120	–1
Nationalist Party –DNVP	52	52	0
People's Party – DVP	11	2	–9
Communist Party – KPD	100	81	–19
Nazi Party – NSDAP	196	288	+92

△ An analysis of the results of the election of March 1933. See page 23 for more information on the parties.

A problem solved

Hitler had hoped for an outright majority in the Reichstag so that he could be sure of passing the one change he wanted above all others: an Enabling Act, so-called because it would enable his cabinet to make laws without consulting the elected members of the Reichstag or even the President. The problem that faced Hitler was that the Weimar constitution required a two-thirds majority vote in the Reichstag in favour of such a major change. The Nazis still did not have that majority, but they found three ways of solving their problem.

1 Göring, who was the presiding officer over the Reichstag, simply announced that he would be ignoring the votes of all Communist members. By refusing to count these votes, a two-thirds majority would be easier to achieve. But Göring had no right under the constitution to discount the Communists' votes in this way. Despite this, in the anti-Communist fever that was gripping the nation, there were few complaints.
2 In the days leading up to the vote on the Enabling Act, Hitler resorted to frightening undecided parties into submission by declaring that if the Act were not passed, the nation would face anarchy. On the face of it he was offering an analysis of just how divided Germany was, but in reality he was letting it be known that the SA would be let loose on the streets in a bloodbath against their enemies if the vote did not go as he wanted.
3 In meetings in the days before the vote, Hitler was negotiating a deal with the Roman Catholic Centre Party. He dealt with their fears by assuring them that he had no plans to ban the Party and he promised not to restrict the rights of the Church.

'You are no longer needed!'

Having prepared the ground, on 21 March Hitler appeared before the newly elected Reichstag, in its temporary home in an opera house at Potsdam just outside Berlin. He put forward his Enabling Act under the name of the Law for Removing the Distress of the People and the Reich. Two days later, when the vote was taken, SA brownshirts stood threateningly in aisles, corridors and in the chamber itself. Members of the Reichstag – Social Democrats, independents and others – had to move past them in order to take their seats. Many chose not to attend and therefore could not vote.

The Nationalist Party had pledged to vote with the Nazis which meant the Nazis needed 31 votes from other Reichstag members. In the end, only one man made a speech against the new law – the leader of the Social Democrats, Otto Wels – but even as he spoke he had a cyanide capsule in his pocket ready to take his own life rather than be arrested and tortured by the SA. He was howled down by the SA and Nazi members with Hitler adding, 'You are no longer needed! – The star of Germany will rise and yours will sink! Your death knell has sounded!'

The vote was counted. 441 voted in support of the new law. Only 94 Social Democrats voted against. Even if the Communists had been allowed to vote against the Act, it would still have passed. Another step on the descent to dictatorship had been taken.

■ Now do the three tasks described on page 37 for this law:

1. Make your notes.
2. Decide whether Hitler was acting legally.
3. Decide whether the Enabling Act should be replaced on the top of the step by some more significant event and justify your decision.

Step 3: The Civil Service Act – 7 April 1933

The Nazis wanted to have full control over as many aspects of German political life as they could. It is no surprise, then, that they quickly turned their attention to the civil service, the men and women whose work it was to carry out the policies and duties of central and local government in cities, towns and villages all over the nation. The German civil service covered a far wider range of activities than it does in Britain. For example, teachers in schools and universities were part of the German civil service.

The changes started at the top. In early February many high-ranking **civil servants** were removed from their posts and were replaced by Nazis. Through SA intimidation or actual violence, many officials resigned their posts without any change in the law having been made but on 7 April 1933 the Act for the Restoration of the Professional Civil Service was passed and this gave a legal basis for the changes. The Act was designed to cleanse the service of any officials who would not follow Nazi beliefs. It required the dismissal of anyone whose former political activities could not guarantee that they would act in the interests of the national (i.e. Nazi controlled) state and any non-Aryans. The Act insisted that these dismissals could take place 'even when there are no grounds for such action under existing law'. This was the first anti-Semitic law to have been passed in Germany since Jews were given full civil rights in 1871.

The most senior **civil service** post, in charge of the affairs of Hitler's office as Chancellor, went to Hans Lammers. Over time he became very close to Martin Bormann and together they controlled who had access to Hitler himself. This gave them great influence in the Third Reich. (Also see page 81.)

One way to avoid being dismissed, of course, was to show loyalty by joining the Nazi Party and well over one million civil servants did exactly that in the first six months of 1933. At the same time others, who would not or could not join the Nazis, resigned their posts. Many academics, including Professor Albert Einstein, moved to continue their careers in the USA or elsewhere.

This law was drastic enough in itself, but it was actually part of an even more pervasive movement that worked its way through German social life from the first months of Nazi rule. The name given by the Nazis for this was *Gleichschaltung*. In many books this is translated as 'co-ordination' as it concerns the drawing together of different groups into one broader system. But the German word itself is also used for electrical circuits where one switch can control everything on the circuit. In other words it may be helpful to think of this movement as 're-wiring' German society.

This co-ordination or re-wiring reached out to all aspects of German life where people formed associations. This ranged from business groups to bee-keeping groups, from sports clubs to choirs, from war veterans to railway workers. Any group or society that wanted to continue had to join official Nazi bodies that incorporated their particular activity. Germans who have looked back on these years wondering why they did not resist have given three main reasons: fear of the consequences, a genuine desire to belong to something powerful, and a naïve hope that they might change Nazism from the inside.

By the middle of 1933, barely any group activity in Germany lay beyond the reach of the Nazi Party, with the exception of the army and the Churches. And, of course, if bee-keeping was to be carefully controlled and constrained, so were political parties and trade unions.

■ Now do the three tasks described on page 37 for this law:

1. Make your notes.
2. Decide whether Hitler was acting legally.
3. Decide whether the Civil Service Act should be replaced on the top of the step by some more significant event and justify your decision.

Step 4: Act to Ban New Parties – 14 July 1933

Communists

Ever since the Reichstag fire and the emergency decree of 28 February 1933, Germany's Communists had effectively been silenced as the Nazis acted to prevent any possible uprising. Hitler's decision not to ban the KPD itself for fear of driving Communist voters into support for the SPD ended with the 5 March elections. On 6 March the KPD was officially banned, and the process began of rounding up and arresting any remaining members. The SA, largely freed from police intervention, now acted often on their own initiative, intimidating, threatening, beating, robbing or simply arresting individuals they believed to be Communists. Where police did try to restrain the SA their efforts were swept aside and those ministers in the federated states who spoke out against SA violence and theft found themselves being removed by Wilhelm Frick. Under the emergency decree, he could claim that these ministers were obstructing the preservation of public order by standing in the way of SA action. He would replace them with hand-picked Nazis.

With the extra powers gained by the passage of the Enabling Act on 24 March, Hitler was now free to take similar action against all political parties, but his first target was the trade union movement, not in itself a political party, but home to many left-wing political activists.

Trade unions

The offices of trade unions had already been attacked in early February 1933. Fearing the possibility of a nationwide strike against Hitler's appointment as Chancellor, the Nazis had arrested many trade union leaders and had closed many trade unionist newspapers. Once again, the left wing did itself no favours as remaining trade union leaders went out of their way to distance themselves from the Social Democrats hoping that this would win favour with the Nazis. In April they held meetings with Göbbels who assured them that the Nazis wanted to put an end to class differences between workers and employers and unite everyone for the common good. He promised to make 1 May an annual holiday in honour of German Labour. Seeing this as a promising sign of better relations, the union leaders agreed.

On 1 May 1933 the streets of Berlin were filled with workers and their marching bands celebrating the first ever 'Day of National Labour'. On 2 May, with no warning, the offices of every left-wing trade union in Germany was raided, their leaders arrested, their newspapers shut down and their banks closed. Their assets and membership fell under the control of the German Labour Front (DAF) and its chief, Robert Ley (see page 59). Strikes were declared illegal. Trade unions had been 'co-ordinated' under Nazi control.

△ A May Day poster from 1933, showing German workers united under the Nazi flag.

Social Democrats

The left-wing Social Democratic Party (SPD) had been the biggest party in Germany since the founding of the Weimar Republic in 1919 and enjoyed considerable support among the German working classes. With the trade unions safely constrained, however, the Nazi leadership now felt confident to attack the SPD without any chance of a left-wing backlash on the streets. They were right. On 10 May the government claimed, with no basis in fact, that there had been corrupt use of SPD funds and seized all its offices and whatever wealth it could lay its hands on. Many Social Democrat leaders fled Germany and although the Party's deputies in the Reichstag continued to attend and to vote, effectively its days were numbered. The final blow fell on 21 June when Wilhelm Frick used the powers of the emergency decree to announce that the SPD must be banned as a dangerous enemy of the German nation. Its deputies could no longer attend the Reichstag, and no further SPD meetings were to be held or publications produced. Over 3000 party workers were arrested, imprisoned and many were tortured. Some were murdered, supposedly 'while attempting to escape'.

... And finally, the rest

■ Now do the three tasks described on page 37 for this act:

1. Make your notes.
2. Decide whether Hitler was acting legally.
3. Decide whether the Act to ban new Parties should be replaced on the top of the step by some more significant event and justify your decision.

Now that their left-wing opponents were all dealt with, you might think that the Nazis would accept the continued existence of other political parties of the centre and the right. But Hitler wanted a one party state. All other parties had to go. The next target was the Centre Party, traditionally the home for Roman Catholic voters and closely tied to that Church.

Rather than try to crush the Roman Catholic Church in Germany as a way of ending the Centre Party, Hitler followed the lead of Italian dictator, Mussolini, and came to a deal with the Pope. Any agreement signed by the Catholic Church with another country is called a Concordat. This one, signed on 1 July 1933, was known as the *Reichskonkordat*. By its terms, Hitler promised not to interfere in the Catholic Church and to allow it to continue to run its various activities in education and community service. In return, the Pope agreed that the Centre Party would be dissolved and the Church would not interfere in politics. But even as the Concordat was being negotiated, any individual Catholics, such as writers, lawyers or journalists, whose views offended the regime, were being arrested and sent to the ever-growing **concentration camps**. On 5 July, the Centre Party formally ended itself and its Reichstag deputies joined the Nazi Party.

For more on the **concentration camps** see page 106.

By then, every other **party** had seen they could not continue and had dissolved themselves one by one. The Nationalist Party (DNVP), Hitler's partners in allowing the Enabling Act to pass through the Reichstag, was pressurised to disband and joined forces with the Nazi Party on 26 June. The Democrats (DDP) followed two days later and on 4 July 1933, the People's Party (DVP), once the party of Gustav Stresemann in the most hopeful era of the Weimar years, disappeared.

See the chart on page 23 for more on these **parties**.

Proud of its victory over all rivals, and free from any opposition, the Nazi regime passed the Act to Ban New Parties on 14 July. Germany was officially a one party state.

Step 5: Act for the Reconstruction of the State – 31 January 1934

By the summer of 1933, within six months of becoming Chancellor, Hitler had tamed trade unionism and had wiped away all other political parties. He had also set in train the process of co-ordination that was re-wiring German life so that the Nazi Party had full control of the nation. In the second half of the year he eased the pace of institutional change, but in January 1934, on the anniversary of his first day as Chancellor, a new law confirmed another important shift that had been under way for months.

Local government in Germany was organised into regions, or *Länder*. Each region elected its own assembly to manage local affairs. This was not a system that Hitler would allow to continue. By 1928, for the purpose of organising his Nazi Party long before he was appointed Chancellor, Hitler had divided Germany into 42 *gaue*, each with a *gauleiter* responsible for local Nazi activity. He decided to use the Party structures and officials instead of the old democratically elected local government system. In March and April 1933 as part of *Gleichschaltung*, provisional laws had given the Chancellor the right to appoint members to the *Länder* without any election and to put in place new Reich Governors. Local government leaders unsympathetic to the Nazis were swiftly removed and the men who replaced them were often Nazi Party *gauleiters*. This system was finally tidied up and made official by the Act for the Reconstruction of the State, passed on 31 January 1934. With this Act, local democracy in Germany was officially dead.

◁ You have already encountered at least one Nazi *gauleiter* in this book. That was Wilhelm Kube who appeared in the photograph on page 36. He was an intense and ambitious man. Rather different was Otto Hellmuth shown here, the *gauleiter* in Mainfranken since 1928. Göbbels described him as 'a most retiring unassuming *gauleiter* in whom one had not too much confidence'.

■ Now do the three tasks described on page 37 for this act:

1. Make your notes.
2. Decide whether Hitler was acting legally.
3. Decide whether the Reconstruction of the State Act should be replaced on the top of the step by some more significant event and justify your decision.

Step 6: The Act to set up the People's Court – 24 April 1934

When Hitler was appointed Chancellor in January 1933, the police and the courts were independent of government, although most had strong right-wing leanings. In the immediate aftermath of the Reichstag fire, however, it became very clear that the separation of government from justice would not last.

On learning that a Communist, Marinus van der Lubbe, was the suspect, Hitler publicly announced that the young Dutchman would be executed for the offence. But van der Lubbe's attack had killed no one (unlike Hitler's own Putsch). His offence was arson, not murder or even manslaughter. When Hitler was told that German law did not allow a death sentence for arson, he simply persuaded President Hindenburg to order that any act of treason or arson committed after Hitler had taken power in January 1933 would now be a capital offence. Bearing in mind this retrospective change in the law at the request of the Chancellor, nothing that follows about the judicial system under the Nazis should surprise you.

By April 1933, with the passing of the Enabling Act, all German judges were required to swear an oath of loyalty to the Nazis. Those who refused were dismissed from their positions, but few refused. This meant that Hitler must have been confident that not only van der Lubbe, but also four other leading Communists would be found guilty of the burning of the Reichstag. These included a leading member of the German Communist Party and Hitler was eager to hold them responsible for the fire. But the judge, to Hitler's alarm, followed very strict rules of evidence and although he found van der Lubbe guilty, he acquitted the others.

Hitler's fury at this decision led him to pass the Act to set up the People's Court on 24 April 1934. By this date, still operating under the Enabling Act which had become by now more or less a new constitution, Hitler could do as he liked. This Act set up a separate People's Court that would take on any crimes of high treason or other serious political offences. It aimed to provide rapid justice 'according to the principles of National Socialism'. Two professional judges would hear the cases, but they were to be assisted by three lay judges chosen from groups such as the SA and SS. As time passed, the number of death penalties imposed by this court rose remorselessly. But even with this court available to them, Hitler and Göbbels decided that some very high profile cases should never come to court, just in case the Nazis should be made to look foolish again as they had in the trial for suspects of the Reichstag fire. For this reason, Ernst Thälmann, Head of the German Communist Party was held without trial for eleven years in a concentration camp before being shot in August 1944.

Below the People's Court a range of similar, local 'Special Courts' was set up to deal with other less serious political offences. Alongside these the regular courts continued, in theory as before, but even they passed increasingly severe sentences as the Nazi grip on society tightened between 1933 and 1945.

■ Now do the three tasks described on page 37 for this act:

1. Make your notes.
2. Decide whether Hitler was acting legally.
3. Decide whether the Act to set up the People's Court should be replaced on the top of the step by some more significant event and justify your decision.

Step 7: The Act concerning the Head of State – 1 August 1934

Threats

△ Ernst Röhm, head of the SA, sitting at his desk in Berlin.

We have reached the final step on Germany's descent into dictatorship. The critical events took place in the summer of 1934, but they had their origins long before that. You have learned how Hitler declared in July 1933, as soon as Germany became a one party state, that the pace of change would be eased. Most Germans must have been relieved, but at least one man was desperately disappointed. He was Ernst Röhm, leader of the SA and the figure whose face was removed from later versions of the photograph you saw on page 36.

Röhm had watched as his SA had grown to become a massive but unruly force in Germany. Its members, the brownshirts, had proved to be invaluable to the Nazi Party from its earliest days. They had quite literally provided the muscle to see the party through the violent street politics of the 1920s and early 1930s. They had also seen through the violent enforcement of Hitler's assaults on Communists, Social democrats, Jews and other so-called public enemies in the first half of 1933. In those six months SA numbers had grown at great speed, swelled by citizens impressed by Nazi success, seeking to establish their own loyalty or simply transferring from other right-wing groups that were no longer allowed to operate. The total SA force at the start of 1934 was over 4 million. But with the arrival of the one party state and Hitler's order that the pace of change must settle, the SA was deprived of an obvious role. This was what disappointed Röhm. And this was what worried Hitler.

News reached Hitler that Röhm was talking of his SA, or part of it, taking over as Germany's official army. The actual army was restricted in size by the Treaty of Versailles to just 100,000 men. Its leaders despised the SA and were keen to curb its power. Their force was far more efficient than Röhm's ill-disciplined and poorly equipped street fighters, so there was a genuine risk that open conflict might break out between them despite the disparity in numbers. This would plunge Germany into chaos once more and threaten Hitler's own position. In early 1934 he won assurances from Röhm that the SA would not act against the army and the tension eased for the time being.

Röhm was not Hitler's only concern in the first months of 1934, however. He was increasingly anxious about the words and actions of Franz von Papen who had been his deputy in the coalition government ever since helping him into power as Chancellor. As you read on page 33, von Papen had intended to use the Nazis to enable him and his fellow conservatives to take effective control while Hitler remained a mere figurehead. Things had clearly worked out differently, especially since the Enabling Act of 24 March. By June 1934 von Papen was openly making speeches suggesting that Nazi policies should be curtailed and that Hitler could not contain the forces he had unleashed, notably the SA. Even Göbbels began to worry that Hitler was allowing events to drift and wondered whether von Papen might lead an army attack on the SA that would end Hitler's leadership of Germany. But Hitler did act, violently and decisively.

The Night of the Long Knives

At the end of June, Hitler ordered the SA leadership to attend a meeting at a lakeside hotel near Munich where Röhm was on leave. They were being set up. Hitler had told Heinrich Himmler to plan a clinical operation to exterminate Röhm and those who supported him. Himmler was only too keen to help, knowing that a weakened SA would increase the power of his own **SS**. Early on the morning of 30 June, Hitler himself burst into Röhm's hotel room with two armed detectives and arrested the SA leader. Meanwhile, throughout the hotel, Röhm's supporters were rounded up by the SS and taken off to concentration camps or murdered in cold blood. Röhm was put in a cell and was given a pistol with the option of killing himself. He refused and was shot at point blank range by two SS officers.

For more on the **SS**, see page 74.

The SA was not Hitler's only target that day. Himmler and his murderous deputy, Reinhard Heydrich, also surprised von Papen, placing him under house arrest and killing his two leading advisers. Hitler's predecessor as Chancellor, General Schleicher, was shot dead. Another who died was Hitler's former Nazi ally, Gregor von Strasser, who might have been prepared to work with von Papen. At least 85 of Hitler's rivals were butchered and over a thousand imprisoned in what became known as the 'Night of the Long Knives'.

Göbbels' propaganda portrayed this brutal operation as a desperate but essential act by Hitler to save Germany. He insisted that Röhm was plotting to overthrow the Nazi government and to take power alongside embittered conservatives such as von Papen, aided by funds from France. If Hitler had not taken such swift action, Göbbels argued, the nation would have been plunged into chaos once more.

In a radio broadcast soon afterwards Hitler declared that:

> If anyone should reproach me and ask me why we did not employ the regular courts to pass sentence, my only answer is this: in that hour, I alone was responsible for the fate of the German nation and was therefore the Supreme Justiciar (judge) of the German People!

No one in Germany's judicial system dared challenge this view.

The Führer

In the aftermath of the events of 30 June 1934, most Germans seemed to accept Göbbels' version of events and thanked Hitler for saving Germany once again from anarchy and widespread violence. The army, with just a few exceptions, was grateful that the SA had been curbed. The SA itself saw numbers decline rapidly, but still was left with quite enough brownshirts to be useful to the Nazi Party in the years ahead.

One person who probably made no sense at all of these events was President Hindenburg. The old general was dying. When Hitler visited his bedside on 1 August, Hindenburg called him 'Your Majesty', seeming to believe that Hitler was the Kaiser. Hitler could see that the end was very near and, later that day, he called together the cabinet. This was the chance to take the final step the Nazi leaders had been working towards. They drew up an Act concerning the Head of State. It proclaimed that, at the very moment that President died, all his powers would be merged with those of the Chancellor under a new title.

That moment came at 9.00 am on 2 August when Hindenburg died in his sleep and Adolf Hitler became Führer or 'Leader' of the German people: a single leader of a single party ruling over a single nation.

A dictator.

■ Now do the three tasks described on page 37 for this act:

1 Make your notes.
2 Decide whether Hitler was acting legally.
3 Decide whether the Act concerning the Head of State should be replaced on the top of the step by some more significant event and justify your decision.

■ Concluding your Enquiry

Now summarise your thinking about Germany's descent into dictatorship by creating a new diagram. Unlike the steps on page 37 your version will be a block graph. Each block will represent the event or issue that you decided was most significant in each section in this enquiry.

1 Label each block in your graph with the event or issue that you decided was most significant in that section of the enquiry. Keep the blocks in the order you have studied them, but change the height of each one according to its overall significance in moving Germany towards dictatorship. The most significant event or issue will be your tallest block in the graph. The least significant will be the lowest of the blocks.
2 Beneath your block graph, explain why you showed the height of your graph as you did. What in your opinion, made each one more or less important in shaping Germany's descent to dictatorship?
3 Finally, summarise what you decided about all the acts you have studied. Was Hitler in any sense justified in claiming that every step of Germany's move to dictatorship was legal and constitutionally justified?

Leni Riefenstahl and the art of propaganda

◁ Leni Riefenstahl preparing to direct a scene from *Triumph of the Will*, at Nuremberg 1934.

Perhaps the most contradictory of all German women in the Nazi State was Helene Riefenstahl, known as Leni (1902–2003). She had studied fine art and ballet and was intending to become a professional dancer before a knee injury put an end to her promising career. Leni moved into films, first acting and then producing and directing. In 1932 she directed her first solo film, *Das Blaue Licht* (*The Blue Light*) which won praise and attracted the attention of Adolf Hitler.

In 1933 Riefenstahl was appointed an adviser to the Nazi Party on films and how the moving image could be used as propaganda. Her two most impressive works were officially documentaries. One showed the annual Nazi Party Congress in Nuremberg in 1934 and the other was about the 1936 Berlin Olympic Games. Both were masterpieces in the use of light, movement, camera angle and photographic techniques, but they were fully exploited by the Nazi Party as propaganda to show the resurgent power of Germany under Hitler.

Riefenstahl's films for the Nazis dogged her career after the war. Years later commenting upon meeting Hitler, Riefenstahl remarked, 'It was the biggest catastrophe of my life'. She went on to add that she would be forever defending her reputation since she did not regard herself as a Nazi or even a supporter of the Nazis, although she was fascinated by them. She was offered the once-in-a-lifetime opportunity to work at the heart of government with every possible resource she needed to make films, where money was no barrier to making films. She always maintained that she never collaborated in the work of the Nazis and was in no way responsible for their crimes. She was briefly held by the Allies at the end of the war on suspicion of committing pro-Nazi crimes, however; all charges were later dropped.

She no longer made films but developed a name for herself taking still images and becoming a photo-journalist. Riefenstahl died shortly after her 101st birthday in Germany.

Triumph Des Willens (*Triumph of the Will*), 1934

The film opens with the Horst Wessel song, the theme of the SA and a second anthem for Nazi Germany, playing in the background. These words appear on the screen:

> On 5th September 1934
> 20 years after the outbreak of the World War
> 16 years after the beginning of German suffering
> 19 months after the beginning of the German rebirth
> Adolf Hitler flew again to Nuremberg to review the columns of his faithful followers

It is believed that Hitler had direct access to the editing process and it is likely that the opening narrative was written by him or a leading Nazi rather than by Riefenstahl herself.

After these words, the camera pans to the clouds high above the city of Nuremberg and follows a plane as it begins to descend. In this way Hitler appears from the skies, a messianic figure, and when he eventually touches down and emerges from the plane, he is greeted by adoring crowds. The film then follows his progress by car through the streets lined with cheering men, women and children, sometimes showing the back of Hitler with his arm raised in the Nazi salute (an unusual camera angle which suggest there was a cameraman either in the back of his car or in a car alongside the Führer's). Eventually it centres on the events in the stadium in Nuremberg recording the audience response with carefully angled shots of the huge numbers attending, as workers march past with shovels in place of rifles. The swastika flags fly and the night sky is lit up by torches, searchlights and fireworks, all to the glory of the Nazi Party and Adolf Hitler.

Olympia (*Olympiad*), 1936

Reportedly made as a documentary about the Berlin Olympics in 1936, this was a powerful propaganda tool promoting the Nazi state and the way in which Hitler had turned Germany around. Noticeable were the ways in which Riefenstahl was able to position cameras around the huge neo-classical stadium to capture the moments when thousands of pigeons were released as the Olympic flag was raised, or the crowd's response to the athletes' parade, or when the flame in the Olympic cauldron ignited. The eruption of the crowd, as athletes from France, Greece and Italy returned the Nazi salute to Hitler, provided a vehicle for the Nazis to demonstrate support from around the world for their authoritarian transformation of the country. As well as events inside the stadium, Riefenstahl had cameras lining the route through central Berlin, under the Brandenburg Gate and down the Unter der Linden, as the Olympic torch was carried by a series of runners – the first time this had ever happened and a tradition that has been continued through to the London Games of 2012. This sequence was shot at a different time and not on the day of the torch relay itself. Such was the access Riefenstahl had to Nazi funding, she could request that scenes be filmed again at enormous cost.

5 What did most to create a People's Community?

▷ A 'One-pot-day' token, 1934. The words at the top mean: 'A gift for a hungry fellow-citizen', in the box: 'Day of the One-pot-meal' and in the circle 'Worth 1 mark'. Note the variety of genders, ages and classes represented.

On the second Sunday of each winter month, from October to March, all Germans were expected to have a simple, cheap meal, a stew that could be cooked in one pot, instead of their usual roast. The money saved was then donated to *Winterhilfe* (Winterhelp). This was a charity, in fact set up under Weimar but taken over by the Nazis, which gave food and clothing to the poor each winter. Huge sums were collected – in the winter of 1935–36 over 30 million marks. This picture shows a token, worth 1 mark. It became a large-scale welfare scheme, but run by the Nazi Party, not the Nazi government. Donations to 'Winterhelp' were collected door-to-door by local Nazi Party members and provided a check on everyone's loyalty to the Nazi system.

Hitler's vision for Germany was to unite the nation. In his own words, from 1934:

> People's Community … means the unity of all vital interests … the soldier and the peasant, the merchant and the academic, the worker and the capitalist … to take the only possible direction to which all purposeful German striving must be headed: towards the nation.

The person who drew the artwork for the picture above tried to portray this unity of purpose by showing, from left to right: a girl, a middle class older man, a worker, a mother and baby, a father, a Nazi, a farmer and a policeman. The recipient is called a 'fellow-citizen'.

Remember how important the comradeship of the First World War was to Hitler (see pages 18–19) and how the People's Community (*Volksgemeinschaft*) was central to Nazism (see page 25).

Hitler was well aware that he had only ever won a maximum of 37 per cent support in democratic elections (in July 1932, see page 30). He believed that he needed to win the support of the other 63 per cent because popularity was the only source of his power as Führer. His vision was that they would unite behind him in this 'People's Community' (*Volksgemeinschaft*). In practice there were five aspects to this:

1 Conflict between classes, between people of different political views, between workers and employers, rural and urban interests, and religious conflict between Protestants and Roman Catholics, had fatally weakened the nation. All these distinctions would be swept away in the new Reich.

2 The Nazi Party was the guardian of this People's Community and Hitler was its undisputed leader. As the Nazi slogan ran: 'Hitler for Germany. All Germany for Hitler.' There was therefore no need for any other political parties. Everybody had to obey Hitler and the Nazi government without doubt or question.

3 Only true Germans could be part of this People's Community, those, as Hitler often put it, of 'pure German blood'. There was therefore no place for people of other races. Nor was there room for those labelled 'community aliens' – the workshy, the drunken, the recidivist criminals. (You will find out in Chapter 8 what happened to all those who could not, or would not, fit this definition of the People's Community.)

4 Everyone had their roles in the People's Community. Children should obey their parents and be good pupils at school. Women should accept that their role was to have babies and look after them and their husbands. Everyone else should work in whatever the Nazi government told them to do, without complaining.

5 As you will discover in Chapter 7, Germany was not a particularly prosperous country. Hitler told the German people that the People's Community would raise their standard of living. As Hitler said: 'I have the ambition to make the German people rich and Germany beautiful. I want to see the living standard of the individual raised.'

Enquiry Focus: What did most to create a People's Community?

In this chapter you will find out how the Nazi government set out to put into effect this People's Community. Hitler knew that he could pass laws and regulations to change people's lives, but, as you can see, creating the People's Community required changing people's attitudes and values. We will begin by exploring **three important methods** that the Nazis used to promote the five aspects of the People's Community above and to change the way people thought. These were:

- **propaganda**
- **fear**
- **popular organisations**.

We will then consider **three important groups** in German society and how the drive towards a People's Community affected them. The groups are:

- **women**
- **young people**
- **workers**.

We can then judge which approach was the most important and will conclude by examining just how deep this People's Community really went.

Propaganda

Hitler and Göbbels were among the first twentieth century leaders to understand the importance of propaganda. Göbbels was quite correct when he said in 1934 'Propaganda was our sharpest weapon in conquering the state and remains our sharpest weapon in maintaining and building up the state'. He was given the entirely new post of Minister of Popular Enlightenment and Propaganda in Hitler's first cabinet and described his intentions very clearly:

> It is not enough for people to be more or less reconciled to our regime … Rather, we want to work on people until they have capitulated to us. The new Ministry has no other aim than to unite the nation behind the ideal of a national revolution.

Mass media such as radio, film and popular newspapers were very new, but Göbbels and Hitler had obviously thought hard about how to use them. What they said is quite revealing of their attitude to democracy and how state-controlled propaganda in mass media would work. Göbbels wrote:

> It is the task of state propaganda to simplify complicated ways of thinking so that even the smallest man in the street may understand.

Hitler was even more explicit:

> The capacity of the masses for understanding is extremely limited and weak. Bearing this in mind, any effective propaganda must be reduced to the minimum of essential concepts, … expressed through a few stereotyped formulae … Only constant repetition can bring success in … instilling ideas into the memory of the crowd.

Göbbels' ministry had the double task of promoting Nazi ideas and successes and eliminating all contrary views in five main media.

1 **The press** From 1933 all newspaper owners, editors and journalists had to be approved by the government. 1300 Jews and known opponents of the Nazis were immediately removed from their jobs. Newspapers were barred from publishing anything which would 'weaken the strength of the Reich abroad or at home, the resolution of the people, German defence or the economy … as well as everything offensive to the honour or dignity of a German'. These are obviously both wide and vague restrictions, but editors were held personally responsible for what they published. A Nazi court could pass harsh sentences on anyone who they decided had broken them.

   The Nazi News Agency provided news stories, which newspapers had to print, with instructions to editors on how much space to give them and on which pages. Editors were also told what they could not publish.

   Gradually an even simpler method of control took place: the Nazi government bought up newspapers and ran them directly. By 1944, 82 per cent of the press was owned by the Nazis.

2 **Radio** German radio began in 1925 and was already in state hands. As with the press, all employees who were Jewish or opponents of Nazism were purged. Göbbels called it 'the spiritual weapon of the totalitarian state'. He had a cheap radio manufactured, the *Volksempfänger* or People's Radio, so that as many people as possible could own one. Seven million were sold. It could only pick up German radio.

3 **Fine art** The Nazis loved paintings like the one on this page: realistic, detailed, telling a story which has a strong Nazi message. Under Ministry control, paintings they disapproved of were not exhibited. In 1937 they even held an 'Exhibition of Degenerate Art', where modernist work, some by famous artists such as Paul Klee, was sneered at and denounced. Sculptors too were expected to toe the Party line, normally by producing works of monumental, heroic Aryans.

△ *The Führer Speaks*, a painting from 1939 by Paul Padua, an artist favoured by the Nazis. Its propaganda content is obvious: the whole family, whatever their age or gender, stops to listen avidly to Hitler on their People's Radio. The portrait of the Leader is pinned to the wall of this humble home, like a religious icon.

4 **Film** The German film industry had an international reputation in the Weimar years and was only gradually brought under Nazi control. Like almost everyone in the world in the 1930s, Hitler and Göbbels loved films, especially Hollywood movies. (Göbbels gave Hitler 18 Mickey Mouse films for Christmas in 1937.) They recognised the entertainment value for the German people, and only about a sixth of the films made under the Nazis had any propaganda content. However, the weekly newsreels which accompanied the main picture were entirely Nazi propaganda. So were, most famously, Leni Riefenstahl's *Triumph of the Will* and *Olympia* (see pages 50–51). Two notorious anti-Semitic films were made, *Jud Süss*, and *The Eternal Jew*. The latter was so gross that audiences were revolted.

5 **Literature** Censorship was strict. Unapproved authors found that publishers would not print their new work and their books were removed from libraries. Nazi fanatics held massive bonfires that burnt banned library books.

Two other aspects of Göbbels work as Director of Propaganda came to dominate the lives of ordinary Germans.

Festivals New festivals were introduced into the calendar. The biggest was Hitler's birthday, on 20 April. Every festival was marked by swastika banners decking all the streets and houses, and processions of uniformed members of Nazi organisations. Failure to show sufficient enthusiasm earned the suspicion of local Party members, always watching for backsliders.

Rallies Photographs like the still below taken from Leni Riefenstahl's *Triumph of the Will*, say it all. Here in the specially-built stadium at Nuremberg, designed by Hitler's favourite architect Albert Speer, thousands of Nazis sink their personal identity and loyally salute their Führer. They revere the so-called 'bloodflag' which was carried at the Beer Hall Putsch in 1923, and touch it like a religious relic with their own flags. The atmosphere is serious, purposeful, dutiful, disciplined, but highly emotional.

The photographic images in every newspaper and every newsreel at the cinema, conveyed the unstoppable power and might of the Nazis, which brooked no dissent.

1 Summarise the ways that the Nazis used **propaganda** to achieve Hitler's vision of a People's Community. You should deal with: the mass media; censorship; festivals; rallies.

2 The People's Community was supposed to have:
- no distinctions of politics or class
- unquestioning support for Hitler and the Nazi Party
- racial conformity
- individuals accepting their role
- improved standards of living.

Which of these aims was promoted most through propaganda?

Fear

If there was fear, who might ordinary Germans be afraid of?

Block wardens The lowest tier of Nazi Party officials were block wardens, numbering about two million by 1939. Their job was to oversee about 50 households each, making sure they paid up for the *Winterhilfe*, hung out swastika banners on Nazi festivals, always gave the Hitler salute, and in general behaved like good members of the People's Community. Their powers were relatively small: they could get a person's welfare benefit stopped, or find someone a better flat. However, they were always there, part of people's everyday lives and it is these little things which make life tolerable or not. Worst of all, they could report suspected opponents of the regime to the Gestapo.

The Gestapo The Gestapo (*Geheime Staatspolizei*) were the state secret police. Set up by Göring in November 1933, they came under Himmler's control in 1936. They operated outside the law, could arrest people without charge, hold them as long as they wished and send them to concentration camps. Often they arrested people straight from prison, having served their sentence, and sent them to a concentration camp.

However, research into Gestapo files has thrown up some interesting facts. For example, far from being a vast secret army of spies, there were relatively few Gestapo staff: the city of Krefeld, for example, with a population the same size as Oxford, had just 14 officers and even Cologne, a city as big as Leeds, only 69. Their main work was in dealing with those who were deemed to be outside the People's Community: in the first few years after 1933, the Nazis' political opponents, then later, anti-socials, Jews, homosexuals and religious dissenters. Not, in other words, ordinary Germans. One historian has calculated that only one per cent of Germans who were neither Jews nor Communists had any dealings with the Gestapo.

You will find out more about who the victims of the Nazis were, and what happened to them, in Chapter 8.

Most of their cases came, not from their own spies, but from information laid by others. Of 825 cases dealt with by the Düsseldorf Gestapo, for example, information for 26 per cent came from the general public, 17 per cent from the regular police, 15 per cent from the Gestapo themselves, 13 per cent from other prisoners, 7 per cent from local government officials and 6 per cent from Nazi Party members such as block wardens. It seems that people were quite prepared to denounce their neighbours, acquaintances or ex-partners to the Gestapo. Here is an example from 1940:

> Ilse Totzke lives next door to us. I noticed the above-named because she is of Jewish appearance. I should like to mention that Miss Totzke never responds to the German Greeting [Heil Hitler]. I gathered from what she said that her attitude is anti-German. To my mind Miss Totzke is behaving suspiciously.

In other places as many as 80 per cent of cases arose from information supplied by the public, and was usually based on personal grudges, rather than on political or racial motives. During the war, 73 per cent of cases of people investigated for listening to the BBC were brought by the public. It seems that people were quite ready to use the system to their own advantage.

However, this doesn't mean that there was no fear. The presence of block wardens, the existence of the Gestapo, knowledge of the concentration camps and what went on in them and the sight of Gestapo beating Jews in the street must have had an impact. In a small survey after the war, of 65 Germans who were asked if they were ever afraid of being arrested by the Gestapo, 20 per cent said 'constantly', 42 per cent said 'occasionally' and only 27 per cent said 'never'. Further, when it came to concern about another member of the family being arrested, the figures rose to 47 per cent, 24 per cent and 16 per cent. As you will discover in Chapter 9, in the last years of the war, Nazi terror extended to virtually everyone. The death penalty was extended to cover 40 new offences and more executions were carried out – 5,191 during the war, compared to 644 in the years 1933–39.

Were the German people forced to fall in with the Nazis' plan for a People's Community through fear of what would happen to them if they didn't? This is not an easy question for historians to answer, working many years afterwards, when other emotions have displaced fear, and people have had time to read and think about the past. It also touches close to the issue of the relationship between the German people and the Nazis: if they were not driven by fear, why did they let it happen?

Interpretations of the significance of fear have changed over the years since 1945.

See pages 8–9 for how interpretations of the People's Community fit into the changing historiography of Nazism.

1945–60s The picture painted in these years was of a people terrified into acquiescence. With spies everywhere, a huge apparatus of police surveillance ensured that no one dared to speak out. 'What was fear? Fear was the Third Reich', as one German is reported as saying. This fitted with a view of the Nazis as people apart from others, carrying out their unspeakable deeds unbeknown to the mass of Germans.

1960s–1980s The assumption in the years immediately after the war was that all records had been destroyed, so the only evidence was the testimony of the German people, who were naturally keen to distance themselves from the Nazis. However, from the 1960s a number of German historians found and began to use records of everyday life in the Nazi years. Martin Broszat ran a major project from 1977–83, studying Bavaria. He showed that, for most people, life carried on as close to normal as they could make it, perhaps with minor acts of resistance and grumbling, but generally keeping out of trouble by neither supporting nor opposing Nazi policy. His former pupil, the British historian Ian Kershaw characterised this: 'The road to Auschwitz was built by hate, but paved with indifference.'

1 Summarise the ways that the Nazis used **fear** to achieve Hitler's vision of a People's Community. In your summary consider whether there really was an atmosphere of fear, giving evidence for and against.

2 The People's Community was supposed to have:

- no distinctions of politics or class
- unquestioning support for Hitler and the Nazi Party
- racial conformity
- individuals accepting their role
- improved standards of living.

Which of these aims could be best achieved through fear?

Popular organisations

Since the 1980s historians have emphasised the efforts the Nazi regime made to win over the German people by providing leisure and entertainment organisations. As Mallman and Paul wrote in 1991:

> Neither propaganda nor terror were totally effective. There were many niches left over in which people could conduct themselves quite normally.

Mass organisations were heavily subsidised by the government to win popular support by providing entertainment, sport and holidays for ordinary German working people.

This is the longest building complex in the world – 4.5 km long – built by the Nazi government, at Prora on the north German Baltic coast. It was intended to provide seaside holiday accommodation for 20,000 workers and their families, with its own restaurants, cinemas, sports halls, heated swimming pool, theatre, railway station and post office. Begun in 1936 as part of the 'Strength Through Joy' programme (see below), it was nearing completion in 1939 when the war started and workers were drafted into the armaments industry.

The German Labour Front (*Deutsche Arbeitsfront* or DAF) was set up in 1933 to remove conflict between workers and employers in the new Nazi state: both sides had to join. Apart from controlling workers' conditions of employment (see page 65), it also provided other benefits through an organisation called Strength Through Joy (*Kraft durch Freude* or KdF). Its head, Robert Ley, described the KdF as 'The shortest formula to which National Socialism for the broad masses can be reduced'.

Every worker was automatically a member through having to be in the DAF (and have money deducted from their pay for it). Nevertheless, with subsidy of 29 million Reichsmarks, it offered a wide range of sporting, cultural and leisure activities at reduced prices. Three million Germans took part in gymnastics and many received cheap coaching in what had been regarded as exclusively middle class sports, such as tennis and sailing. By 1938, 2.5 million Germans had taken up cheap seats at concerts, 6.5 million at the opera and 7.5 million at theatres – many of which were newly built.

There were subsidised holidays as well. More than half of German workers had never been away on holiday: by 1938 over 10 million workers were going on KdF holidays, and if the complex at Prora had been finished it would have been many more. KdF also owned eight cruise liners, and 1.7 million Germans saw new lands and people as a result. The cruise liners were all one class, and the intention was partly to educate German workers about the world, and partly to make clear to them their racial superiority.

There was even the offer of a car, the 'Strength Through Joy car', later called the People's Car or Volkswagen. A worker saved 5 marks a week and would receive a Volkswagen when they were ready. (In fact, none were produced until after the war.) Yet another organisation with a fancy name, Beauty of Labour (*Schönheit der Arbeit*), did a great deal to improve the working environment, providing canteens, showers, lockers and so on. The workers, however, had to provide unpaid labour for these improvements.

These KdF activities were not entirely successful. Workers often found themselves in the cheaper seats, or given worse rooms and inferior food to other guests at hotels. The biggest users of many of its cheap offers were the salaried, middle class employees. Class tensions were not overcome. Nevertheless, many Germans, after the war, remembered their KdF holidays with affection.

1 Summarise the ways that the Nazis used **popular organisations** to achieve Hitler's vision of a People's Community.

2 The People's Community was supposed to have:
- no distinctions of politics or class
- unquestioning support for Hitler and the Nazi Party
- racial conformity
- individuals accepting their role
- improved standards of living.

Which of these aims could be best achieved through popular organisations?

Now that you have studied the three approaches used by the Nazis in creating their 'People's Community', it is time to carry out the three case studies. Each of the following sections explores the lives of people in a particular group in German society and how the drive towards a People's Community affected them. The groups are workers, young people and first of all, women.

Women

The Nazi Party were very clear about women's role in the People's Community: to stay at home and produce babies for the German race. The message was put across in propaganda images like the magazine cover below, and in speeches by Nazi leaders.

If the man's world is said to be the state, his struggle, his readiness to devote his power to the service of the community, then the woman's is a smaller world. For her world is her husband, her family, her children, her home. The greater world is built on the foundation of this smaller one. (Hitler, in 1934)

... the highest service which a woman may perform for the continuation of the nation is to bear racially healthy children. Be happy, good women, that you have been permitted to perform this high duty for Germany! (Hess, 1939)

It needs to be said at this point that gender discrimination was widely practised across the world at this time. Unequal pay was the norm and there was pressure on married women to give up work during the 1930s' unemployment crisis. Before the Nazis even came to power, the German civil service had been instructed to give preference to men over women in job applications. The Nazis just took things further – much further.

▷ Cover picture from *Women Wait* – 'The only official party magazine for women.' The woman is shown holding a baby and told to 'wait', while men do the fighting and farming. In fact lots of German women worked outside the home, especially on peasant farms.

From 1936, women were barred from serving as lawyers or judges, hospital consultants or members of the Reichstag. Only 10 per cent of university places were open to women, and girls were not to be taught Latin, necessary for university entrance.

These changes in the law affected mainly middle class women, who had benefited most from the considerable progress towards gender equality achieved under Weimar. Much wider in its impact was the Marriage Loan Scheme, introduced in 1933 and taken up by a third of all married couples by 1936. When a couple got married they could apply for a loan of up to 1000 Reichsmarks on condition that the woman gave up her job, and did not seek work until the loan was paid off. Of course, this was a Nazi scheme, so there were obstacles: the couple had to prove they were Aryans, that they were not Communists, vagrants or alcoholics, and take a medical test to prove they were not carrying a hereditary disease.

See Chapter 7 for the economic impact of this policy.

There were medals for motherhood: bronze for 4–5 children, silver for 6–7 and gold for 8 (or more!). Childless couples paid higher taxes, childlessness was grounds for divorce and abortion was made more difficult. (Although for women who were racially or socially 'undesirable', abortion was made a lot easier to access.)

As in so many other ways, the regime's policy on women grew more extreme during the war. In Himmler's *Lebensborn* (Spring of Life) project, 'racially pure' girls, 60 per cent of whom were unmarried, had babies by SS men in what was virtually a state brothel. About 8000 babies were born under this scheme.

There were advantages to women in this Nazi emphasis on healthy breeding. Women received health advice and extra rations. Money was spent on improving sanitation in rural areas. Good childcare facilities were provided. Infant mortality rates fell. The women's welfare organisation NSV provided jobs and careers for women who were excluded from other worthwhile jobs.

However, as with several of the aims of the ideal People's Community ideal, there were clashes and contradictions, both with how people wanted to live their lives and with other Nazi aims. In this case, German women had always worked much more than women in, for example, Britain. As Chapter 7 explains, Germany was a more backward country than Britain. In areas with small peasant farms, women made up 60 per cent of the workforce. Six million German women worked in agriculture. (The equivalent figure for Britain was 100,000.) Far from being driven, or persuaded, to stay at home, the number of married German women working went up under the Nazis, from 4.2 million in 1933 to 6.2 million in 1939. There were plenty of jobs in the factories by the late 1930s as the economy recovered, and women were keen to take them.

■ Summarise the ways **women's lives** changed under the Nazis.

In what ways did they NOT change?

Were women most affected by propaganda, fear or popular organisations? Use evidence from this section to support your answer.

Once the war had started, the Nazis' over-riding aim was armaments production and replacing the men who had left the workforce to become soldiers. Some leading Nazis, notably Göbbels, wanted to declare 'Total War' and mobilise every adult in Germany for the war effort. Hitler, sticking to his views about the purely domestic role of women, refused. Britain conscripted women from 1942, but it was not until a year later, with the war already turning against them, that Hitler gave way. Women aged 17–45 were directed to a workplace, although there were lots of exemptions. The figures can be misleading: by 1944, 41 per cent of all British women were conscripted, but 51 per cent of all German women. In Germany, however, many of these women were still in non-military jobs, like farming and domestic service.

Young people

If the Nazis' aim was to create a People's Community with the support of every single German, then winning over the next generation of Germans was a high priority. Hitler was clear what he wanted:

> We older ones are used up ... But my magnificent youngsters! ... With them I can create a new world. My teaching is hard. Weakness has to be knocked out of them ... A violently active, dominating, intrepid, brutal youth ... I will have no intellectual training. (Hitler, quoted by Hermann Rauschning)
>
> In our eyes the German boys of the future must be slender and supple, swift as greyhounds, tough as leather and hard as Krupp steel. (Hitler at Nuremberg, 1934)
>
> The chief purpose of school is to train human beings to realise that the state is more important than the individual, that individuals must be willing and ready to sacrifice themselves for Nation and Führer. (Bernard Rust, Education Minister)

To fulfil these intentions, the Nazi government took over most of a young person's life, both in school and outside it.

In school

All teachers were expected to join the Nazi Teachers League, where they received propaganda and training in Nazi ideology, where and how to put it into practice in the curriculum. Opportunities to do this entered every subject: chemistry lessons were focused on chemical warfare and explosives; biology was about race and the superiority of Aryans; geography was about Germany's need for *lebensraum* (living space). History lessons featured uncritical accounts of Germany's glorious past, its heroes and the iniquity of the '**stab in the back**' of 1918. New textbooks were issued and had to be used. The Hitler salute had to be used at the beginning of each lesson. There were two hours of PE every day. As you would expect, gender differences were strong: boys learned military skills, girls were taught needlework and housecraft. Teachers whose views were unacceptable, or who were Jewish, were sacked; so were many women. By 1936, 30 per cent of all schoolteachers were Nazi Party members.

For the 'stab in the back' myth, see page 11.

It was the same at university level where 1200 university staff were sacked, 33 per cent on racial and 56 per cent on political grounds. The Nazis were actively anti-intellectual – Hitler does not hide his contempt in the first quotation above. All students had to do a year's manual labour before going to university; this included hours of Nazi lectures, most of which they had heard many times before in school or the Hitler Youth. Nazi speakers often took opportunities to humiliate clever students. The number of university students halved between 1933 and 1939, although this was reversed in the war as Hitler realised that he was losing the scientific war of inventions with military applications – such as the atom bomb.

In 1933 élite schools, National Political Education Institutions, (or 'NaPoLAs'), were set up. They were boarding schools, mainly for boys, run by SS and SA officers, to train those who would run the Third Reich in the future. There were sixteen NaPoLAs by 1939.

Out of school

The Hitler Youth movement had been founded in 1926 and had just 20,000 members by 1932. There were other larger youth organisations run by churches and political parties. As soon as the Nazis came to power, all other youth organisations were closed down (except for the Catholic youth organisation which survived until 1936). By 1934 there were 3.5 million members of the Hitler Youth, by 1939 8.7 million. You could join at the age of 6 as a *pimpf* (a rascal); then boys proceeded through the *Deutsches Jungvolk* (German Youth) (10–14) to the Hitler Youth (14–18). The girls' equivalent organisations were the *Jung Mädel* (Young Girls' League) (10–14) and the *Bund Deutscher Mädel* (League of German Maidens) (14–18). Membership was virtually compulsory – parents of non-members were criticised and came under suspicion from block wardens. In this way the Nazi state was replacing the family – whose values were beyond state control – in the bringing up of young people.

The big attraction of these organisations was their activities such as hiking trips, camping, sing-songs, sport – they took over virtually all sporting facilities. As at school, gender played a large part in what kinds of activities you were expected to do: boys practised throwing hand grenades while girls did the cooking and washing up. But there was also a strong indoctrination element too, from the oath: 'I promise always to do my duty in the Hitler Youth, in love and loyalty to the Führer', to lectures on fitness and health, obedience, race and patriotism. Under the leadership of Baldur von Schirach the organisations became increasingly militaristic, always led by adults. Young people began to resent the physical endurance feats they had to undergo, the boring talks and incessant propaganda. They wanted some time to themselves, to have some control over their own lives. Parents resented the inroads these movements made into family life.

Summarise the ways **young people's** lives changed under the Nazis.

In what ways did they NOT change?

Were young people most affected by propaganda, fear or popular organisations? Use evidence from this section to support your answer.

Workers

Winning over German workers to the People's Community was in many ways the Nazis' hardest task. For a start, they made up 46 per cent of the population; further, the Nazis' bitterest enemies, the Communists and the Social Democrats, had drawn most of their support from this class. Nevertheless, there is often considerable working class support for right-wing parties in democracies and in fact 31 per cent of Nazi voters were from that class. So indeed were many Nazi Party members, especially in the SA. The word 'socialist' was in the name of the Party and many members took this seriously.

However, there were contradictions too. To achieve the level of rearmament he wanted for Germany, Hitler knew that he had to gain the support of big business and employers. With characteristic ruthlessness he set about bringing workers and their organisations under Nazi control. **Trade unions** were banned in May 1933 and their assets confiscated. The German Labour Front, (DAF – see above), was set up immediately, bringing employers and workers into one body, under Nazi control. The attack on the SA in the **Night of the Long Knives** in June 1934, fatally weakened the socialist elements in the Nazi movement.

For more on the banning of **trade unions** see page 43.

For more on the **Night of the Long Knives** see page 48.

The DAF, under Robert Ley, was the largest organisation in the Reich, with 7000 employees and 135,000 volunteer workers. Virtually all employers and workers had to join, and it had 22 million members by 1939. There is no doubt that the DAF favoured employers at the expense of employees. Wages were frozen at 1933 levels. While employers got rich from Nazi support for their businesses, real wages remained below the level of 1928 for the whole of the 1930s. Working hours increased to 50 or even 60 hours a week. With no organisation to co-ordinate workers' grievances, strikes were impossible, and anyway illegal. Every worker had to have a workbook, in which employers might put critical comments. Workers were also not allowed to change jobs without permission. Employees who caused employers problems were threatened with being handed over to the Gestapo. In these ways the German working class was brought under Nazi control.

However, there were some major compensations for the working class. In 1933, what every German worker wanted above all else was a job and the Nazis succeeded in creating them. There were 6 million unemployed in Germany in 1932; this had dropped to 35,000 in 1939. There were lots of opportunities for overtime work, paid at normal rates plus 25 per cent. Workers were not free, but at least they had some money in their pockets.

Summarise the ways **workers' lives** changed under the Nazis.

In what ways did they NOT change?

Were workers most affected by propaganda, fear or popular organisations? Use evidence from this section to support your answer.

Concluding your Enquiry

Look at the notes you have made as you analysed the methods the Nazis used to create their People's Community (propaganda, fear and popular organisations) and how these affected the groups in our case studies (women, young people and workers).

Use a table like the one below to summarise your judgements. Put a number of ticks in the box according to the importance of that method for that group: three for very important, down to none for no importance at all.

	PROPAGANDA	FEAR	POPULAR ORGANISATIONS
Women			
Young people			
Workers			

Use your completed table and the evidence from your summaries to write a persuasive argument to say which method seems to you to have been the most influential overall. Don't forget to consider the other methods used.

There is often discussion of 'opposition' to the Nazis; but after late 1933 there was no real opposition. There was, however, resistance, which is the term we prefer to use.

Post-script: Successful?

How can we measure whether the Nazis' attempt to create a People's Community was successful or not? One obvious way is to look at the extent of opposition and resistance to the Nazi government.

The only time when Hitler might have been opposed was in 1933, in the first few months after he had come to power. But, as you saw in Chapter 4, he acted with rapid, violent ruthlessness, smashing opposition organisations, locking up political opponents in concentration camps, unknown numbers of whom were beaten up and even killed. After that many Social Democrats and Communists went into exile. Those that were left were reduced to dropping leaflets and writing slogans on walls. Most of the efforts of the Gestapo went into finding and arresting them. The Nazi response to any opposition was always extreme violence: in 1942, after a group planted a bomb in an anti-Soviet and anti-Semitic exhibition in Berlin, 30 people were arrested and 15 executed. The *Rot Kappelle* (Red Orchestra), a group of mainly Communist intellectuals, was betrayed in 1942 and at least 50 people put to death.

But for most of the 1930s Hitler was genuinely popular. He had been legally appointed, unemployment was falling fast, Germans could have pride in the armed forces again, 'layabouts and the workshy' were being taught a lesson. Emmi Bonhöffer, sister-in-law of Dietrich Bonhöffer (see below), commented many years later:

> There was no resistance movement and there couldn't be. Nowhere in the world can develop a resistance movement when people feel better from day to day. Resistance: we were stones in a torrent and the water crashed over us.

So any form of open resistance required great bravery. There were nine plots to assassinate Hitler, but in only two cases did the bombs actually go off, both failing to kill their target. (For more on the 1944 bomb plot, see page 129.) The White Rose Group was a loose association of a small group of students and some professors centred around Munich University. They objected to the Nazis' actions on religious and moral grounds and published leaflets exposing the Nazis' euthanasia programme (see pages 107–108), as well as German atrocities against Jews and in Poland. They accused the German people of cowardice in not speaking out: 'Isn't it true that every honest German is ashamed of his government these days?' and 'The German people slumber on in dull, stupid sleep and encourage the fascist criminals'. Leaders of the group, Christoph Probst, Hans and Sophie Scholl, were arrested, tried and executed in February 1943.

The Roman Catholic Church tried to ignore the Nazis and care for their own members but there were some acts of open resistance. Bishop Galen of Münster spoke out against the euthanasia campaign. Even refusing to use the Heil Hitler greeting, which was almost compulsory, and preferring the traditional Roman Catholic *Grüss Gott* (God greet you) was a kind of resistance.

Some Protestants, the 'German Christians', supported the Nazis, with 'the swastika on our breasts and the cross in our hearts'. This led a breakaway group of Protestants, the Confessional Church, to leave the official Reich Church in 1934. Dietrich Bonhöffer was a leading figure in the Confessional Church and pointed out the anti-religious nature of Nazism, particularly of the near-worship of the Führer. He was arrested in 1943 and killed in a concentration camp just a month before the end of the war. Another Confessional Church pastor was Martin Niemöller. Arrested and tried in 1937, he was acquitted, but seized by the Gestapo and imprisoned in a concentration camp until the end of the war.

Young people found ways of expressing their hostility to the boring, controlling, regimentation of their schools and the Hitler Youth. 'Swing' groups of rich young people met to hold parties, listen to jazz (which the Nazis hated), wear British fashions and talk English. The name Edelweiss Pirates was given to several groups of working class teenagers. They wore distinctive clothes, went on their own camps, made up, and sang their own anti-Nazi, pro-freedom songs. Such behaviour was a kind of resistance, particularly when they mocked, or attacked, Hitler Youth members. Several Edelweiss Pirates were executed in the last, fanatical months of the war, in Cologne.

But lack of much overt resistance doesn't necessarily mean many people supported the People's Community. With such total control, many people retreated into their family life. Historians have suggested that many minor actions should be seen as forms of resistance. Discussing Nazi atrocities and corruption with friends, continuing to trade with Jews and use Jewish shops, telling anti-Nazi jokes, listening to the BBC, 'going slow' at work, could all be interpreted in this way. When the Allies captured German soldiers they found that younger Germans were more pro-Nazi than their parents. In a survey of German people after the war, 55 per cent of them admitted that they had supported National Socialism at the time; this figure broke down to 75 per cent of men and 47 per cent of women. The Third Reich only lasted 12 years; in time more and more young people would have been indoctrinated into Nazi ideology and accepted the kind of People's Community which was Hitler's vision for them.

■ Bearing in mind the work you did in the first parts of this enquiry, are you surprised by what you have read in this summary of how far Hitler was successful in creating a People's Community?

Letters to the Führer – a historian's insight

To help you understand more about how the German people responded to Nazi dictatorship, we turned to Victoria Harris who is a research fellow in modern European history at the University of Birmingham. She has written and edited books and articles on everyday life in the Third Reich. She also acted as a historical consultant for this book.

You can read Victoria's own summary of her research on pages 70 to 71. But first we wanted to know more about why Victoria became a historian of the Third Reich and her participation in new debates over to what extent the Nazi takeover changed life for ordinary Germans, and what role those citizens played in the functioning of the regime.

Q What first attracted you to German history?

A In 2009 I was asked this question by Professor Sir Richard Evans for his book *Cosmopolitan Islanders*. I am curious to see how my answer might have changed – have I rewritten my own history?

Then, I wrote that 'studying Germany helped me understand the historical context I found myself in, and since I had no personal ties to Germany, it was a far less combative way to do it than exploring either of my own national contexts' (British expat in America).

This answer still feels true. Being an outsider is very helpful in historical research. We are all separated by time from the period we study, but a geographical or national separation allows one to view things more impartially. Germany particularly interests me because, while I don't believe the theory that it took a 'special path' through modern history, its social framework is distinct from that of the UK or USA. Understanding these distinctions helps me better understand both Germany and my two homelands.

Q And why Nazi Germany?

A When I first started studying modern German history at university I became fascinated by how twelve short years of a country's history could overshadow two full centuries. As a professional historian, I began to focus more on the period surrounding the Third Reich in order to examine whether historical and popular focus on this period was a fair representation of the most significant moments in Germany's modern history – particularly as experienced by ordinary people.

Q Is it fair? To what extent did life change for ordinary Germans when the Nazis came to power?

A When I began my first book, on the sex trade in twentieth century Germany, I argued forcefully that life did not change very much at all for Germans in 1933. In part that was because many of the daily realities for ordinary, working-class women such as prostitutes continued unchanged, and the immediate ramifications of the Nazi seizure of power seemed to affect them less than other changes, particularly economic changes. I wanted to oppose the dominant historical view that *everything* changed in 1933. Now I take a more middle ground – viewing 1933 as one of several turning points during this period, together with the inflation of 1923, the onset of the Great Depression in 1929/30, changes in social policy in the mid 1930s, and the loss of Stalingrad in 1943. All these moments changed life for ordinary Germans. But they didn't change all aspects of life for all Germans. It is a continuing problem in our understanding of history that 1933–1945 stands so separate. It helps us more to weigh up these changes and continuities. It is too easy to view a change of regime, or the imposition of a dictatorship as a total break with the past. But this doesn't help us fully understand it.

Q You recently edited a collection of letters to Hitler, written before and during his time in power, and sent by a variety of individuals living both inside and outside of Germany. How did this project change your view of life under the Nazis?

A These letters reveal the complicated relationship Hitler had with his supporters – and also his enemies. They also demonstrate that despite his dictator status, Hitler could not act without first gaining popular support. I was really surprised by how much German citizens complained to Hitler about things – and how often those letters were answered!

In this book I wrote:

'In establishing a successful dictatorship, Hitler needed his people. And needed to establish a dialogue with them. If he was to convince them that he had the answers for Germany, in return he had to listen to their problems, accept their advice, and respond to their concerns – or at least appear to. The secret to the Third Reich's success during its height in the 1930s and early 1940s was Germans' sense that they could engage in a conversation with their leader, and that he was in some way listening.'

Q Why is the Third Reich still so important for us to understand today?

A Nazi Germany stands as a sobering reminder of how our actions now may be judged differently by our children and grandchildren, and how relatively powerless we are as individuals to change much of the injustice taking place in today's world. It's easy to look back at ordinary Germans and think 'why didn't they *do* anything?' We need to also ask, 'would we have done any better?' and also 'could we do better now, today?'

Letters to the Führer – a historian's insight

Victoria Harris summarises some findings from her book, *Letters to Hitler* (Polity Press: 2011).

The appointment of Hitler as Chancellor on 30 January 1933 is rightfully viewed as a major political turning point in Germany's modern history. What is more difficult for historians to assess, however, is the degree to which the Nazi Party's subsequent seizure of power and creation of a dictatorship affected the everyday life of ordinary Germans.

All Germans were of course affected by the sweeping changes to government Hitler and his party made in their first hundred days in power, and perhaps more so by the various political, social and economic changes that took place within the first eighteenth months of the Third Reich. Certain Germans were affected more than others, with Jewish and Communist citizens, for example, as well as minority religious groups such as the Jehovah's Witnesses, facing immediate infringements on their freedoms. However, for many other Germans, business continued as usual. Indeed for some, 1933 was probably far less shocking than either the Great Depression of 1933 or the end of the First World War back in 1918.

In order to explore the question of what life was like under the Third Reich, historians are increasingly seeking out personal documents from ordinary people – in other words, not important Nazi functionaries, the very wealthy nor those strongly opposed to Nazism. One useful source is proving to be the many letters Germans wrote to Hitler himself. In these letters historians can assess how Germans felt about Hitler's rule, what they considered to be the most important issues of the day, and to what extent they supported Nazi propaganda. Do the Nazi Party and German citizens' views of life after 1933 match up?

We know that after Hitler took power, his office had to hire four new employees to deal with the volume of post and gifts arriving on his desk. This tells us that many Germans felt his seizure of power to be significant. But while some of the letters were congratulatory – or even obsessive – many offered suggestions, sought personal favours, or even openly criticised the party. All of them expected to be answered. While Hitler had encouraged this kind of cultish behaviour, he had clearly not succeeded in cultivating blind obedience.

For example, teacher Wilhelm Becker wrote to Hitler's half sister and housekeeper on 18 December 1933 with a package of Christmas cards from his pupils. So far this sounds like relatively ordinary devotion. He then made a demand, albeit politely, writing: 'Your brother will certainly take a few days off from the exertions of political life and seek rest and relaxation in the stillness of your mountain landscape ... lay the portfolio before him during some leisure hour.'

When he had not received a reply by 23 January 1934, he wrote again, pushing for a response. We know from his letters that Wilhelm Becker supported Hitler, that the Nazi takeover was a positive change for him. We also know that he wrote to Hitler in a way he may have written to any ordinary politician, or even perhaps a business leader or colleague. He had a request, and when it was not fulfilled satisfactorily, he followed it up – with no fear of reprisal. (*Letters to Hitler*, pp. 85–88)

Other Germans saw Hitler's arrival as presenting new business opportunities, more than anything else. Fritz Dittrich, for example, wrote to Hitler before he took power in May 1932, proposing a Hitler branded cigarette and cigar. When his request was denied by the anti-smoking Hitler, he wrote again, noting that 'in England "Prince of Wales" and "Lord so-and-so" were very successful brands of cigarettes.' Fritz Dittrich wanted to use Hitler for his own gain; he was not frightening or unapproachable, he was an opportunity. What's more, this letter, which was written before 1933 is very similar to some written after, revealing that Hitler's seizure of power did not particularly change life for Germans, even in cases where their lives directly related to Hitler. (*Letters to Hitler*, pp. 60–62)

Three further letters reveal even greater surprises about life under the Third Reich in the 1930s. The first letter was sent by Editha

Badke from Berlin on 25 March 1934. It was the third time she had written to Hitler regarding her husband's disappearance (*Letters to Hitler*, p. 126):

'Dear Mr Reich Chancellor!

I am writing to you for the third time. It cannot be true that you are not willing to listen to my request. No, I assume that you did not personally receive my letters of 16 January and 26 February of this year, otherwise I would have received a reply. But the torment increases from month to month. How can it be that my husband has already been imprisoned for five months without any prospect of a trial? If he had committed a serious offence, I could understand this; but as it is it is, incomprehensible to me. He has always been co-operative, and everyone who knows him can give him a good recommendation. I assure you again and again, that we are willing to accept whatever you give us. We also do not want to complain that in this year we have still not found work, because it is certainly very, very hard to provide jobs for millions of people who are unemployed. I grant that in their need people are often indignant. But when there are all kinds of things to buy and I have no money and [one] has known only poverty ever since childhood, then one does have doubts. But I have recovered my trust in a better future, and therefore I am willing to accept everything, only I ask you, be lenient and give my husband his freedom back.

With great confidence and thanks I remain, with a German salute Editha Badke'

Editha Badke's husband may well have already been dead by this time – perhaps this is why her letters were not answered. While the sad fate of her husband fits with our views of Nazi Germany, Editha's confidence in writing to Hitler not once, but three times, protesting his disappearance, is not necessarily something we would have expected to be possible within this dictatorship.

The second critical letter was written in 1934 by Berlin artist Rudolk Jaenicke, who had been a Nazi supporter since 1932. He wanted to work as a party official, but a Jewish grandmother was discovered in his ancestry, and his request was denied. Despite being revealed as Jewish under Nazi law, Jaenicke was determined to work for the Nazis and also determined to fight for his rights. He wrote: 'We are also people and perhaps better than some others. Must I leave the Nazi Party, etc.? I can't see why.'

Amazingly, Hitler's private office replied to this letter. Rudolf Jaenicke's letter reveals several fascinating facts – first that life had indeed changed for Germans who were Jewish. Second, that, despite these changes, German Jews were so well assimilated that many, including Jaenicke, found it possible to still support the Nazi Party. Third, because of their support for the Nazis despite their discrimination against Jews, we can see that Germans were able to take on board certain aspects of Nazi ideology while ignoring others that they did not like – or that the Nazis were not yet so consistently vocal about their anti-Semitism. Fourth, and most amazingly, we can see that the Nazis were not yet confident – or aware – enough of their plans to destroy 'Jewry', or indeed their political power, that they still thought it necessary to answer a letter from a Jew. These contradictory findings confuse the debate between functionalist historians, who have argued that Nazis developed policy as they went along, and intentionalists, who have said that Hitler and his party had hatched their plans far in advance. (*Letters to Hitler*, pp. 142–43)

Still further confusing this debate, and revealing the degree to which Germans were untouched by Nazi militarisation during the 1930s, is a letter from a couple in 1938. At this time Hitler was preparing for war. But his citizens were either unaware of this, or refused to believe it. Josef and Elli Jablonski were no exception, writing: 'It makes us happy and glad to know that peace exists and will remain.' (*Letters to Hitler*, p. 180) So comfortable were most Germans during the 1930s, they most certainly did not want war. One of the biggest changes for Germans during this period was a sense of economic, political and also social stability. Whether the Nazis brought this is still up for debate. But they were not prepared for this to be shattered by war. It was this unwanted war that dramatically changed life for ordinary Germans, and made the charismatic and persuasive Hitler increasingly unpopular.

6 Der Führer: What sort of dictator was Adolf Hitler?

△ 'One People, one Empire, one Leader!' A Nazi poster from 1938.

In Chapter 3 we saw that Hitler was ushered into power by the conservative nationalist élites who expected to control him. Instead, as we saw in Chapter 4, he had made himself dictator of Germany within eighteen months of becoming Chancellor. In Chapter 5 we explored how he used his extraordinary powers to set about changing the way the German people thought and behaved. His position in the Nazi Party, the government and the nation was unassailable and remained so right to the bitter end in 1945. Indeed, some have argued that Nazism was really just 'Hitlerism'. This therefore seems the right point in this book to examine his role as dictator.

Yet there are some puzzles lurking in this question. Writers and historians have disagreed over whether he was genuinely popular, and how exactly he governed Germany. Here are two examples of their views:

> Few if any, twentieth century political leaders have enjoyed greater popularity among their own people than Hitler in the decade or so following his assumption of power on 30 January 1933. (Ian Kershaw, *The Hitler Myth*, 1987)

> In the twelve years of his rule in Germany Hitler produced the biggest confusion in government that has ever existed in a civilised state. (Otto Dietrich, Hitler's Press Chief, *Twelve years with Hitler*, 1955)

For the first 30-odd years of his life Adolf Hitler was not liked by his family, schoolmates and pre-war Vienna acquaintances. How could he become the highly popular figure Kershaw describes? And how could the extraordinarily dynamic actions of the Nazi government as well as Hitler's personal popularity emerge from the chaotic situation Dietrich describes? And what is the link, if any, between these two aspects of Hitler's dictatorship?

■ **Enquiry Focus**: What sort of dictator was Adolf Hitler?

Just as there two sides to a coin like the Nazi Pfennig (penny) shown here, there were two sides to Hitler's dictatorship. You will be considering each side in turn as you work towards your answer to the enquiry question.

A – Hitler's personal popularity

B – Hitler's part in the government of Germany

Historians must choose their words carefully. This enquiry requires you to analyse these two aspects of Hitler's dictatorship. At intervals we will ask you to select just two words or phrases to capture the essence of your conclusions about him. The list below offers a range of suggestions you might wish to use. But bear in mind the fact that we have included some that we think would be sensible choices as well as some that are less likely to be relevant. At each stage you can also suggest words or short phrases of your own if you think you have better ideas. Just be sure that you can use the evidence from the enquiry to support your choice of words, whatever they are. You may find that using just a few words is harder than using many!

Words you might wish to use to capture the essence of Hitler's dictatorship:

Adored	Admired	Loved	Heroic
Devoted	Disorganised	Overwhelmed	Exciting
Inspiring	Lazy	Erratic	Great
Simple	Genius	Manipulative	Fanatical
Pure	Normal	Careful	Masterly
Nice	Feared	Approved	Clever

Erich **Lüdendorff**, 1865–1937 was a hero as a result of his successes as a First World War general. After the war he turned to far-right politics and for a time supported the Nazis.

Julius **Streicher**, (1885–1946) was a fanatical anti-Semite, publisher of *Der Stürmer* and early Nazi Party member.

SS (Schützstaffel) started as Hitler's personal bodyguard of picked SA men. Himmler was given command of the SS in 1925 and turned it into a huge separate organisation of the most fanatical and dedicated Nazis.

Hitler's personal popularity

Early popularity with the Nazi Party

It took time for Hitler to emerge as the adored leader of Germany. If the 1923 Beer Hall Putsch had succeeded, the war-hero **Lüdendorff**, and not Hitler would have become Chancellor. But already Hitler's charisma as a speaker had begun to work on members of his own Party. Not only the dim and mentally unstable Hess, but also Himmler, Göring, **Streicher**, Ley (see page 65) and Göbbels all devoted themselves to him from 1922/23 onwards.

Göbbels wrote in his diary in 1925:

> Adolf Hitler, I love you because you are both great and simple at the same time. What one calls a genius.

Early converts to Nazism describe hearing Hitler for the first time; it was like a religious conversion:

> There was only one thing for me, either to win with Adolf Hitler or to die with him. The personality of the Führer had me totally in its spell.

> Whenever I worked for the Movement and applied myself for our Führer, I always felt there was nothing higher or nobler I could do for Adolf Hitler and thereby for Germany, our people and Fatherland.

Other aspects of the cult of leadership started around this time: the title of Führer (Leader), the personal bodyguard, the **SS** and the salute, made compulsory throughout the Party from 1926.

Popularity and propaganda

Before the early 1930s Hitler was, to most Germans, a rather strange and irrelevant Bavarian fanatic, with floppy hair and a funny moustache. It was the presidential election of 1932 and the successes of the Nazis in the Reichstag elections which made him a national figure who had to be taken seriously. Hitler's appointment as Chancellor in January 1933 and particularly the March 1933 election victory, gave Göbbels his opportunity to really start promoting him. Regular, massive and well-reported rallies and commemorative celebrations meant that the cult of Hitler now went outside the Party to the whole nation. From 1933, his birthday on 20 April was a signal for outpourings of enthusiasm. Every town had bunting across the streets, shop window displays and processions.

Hitler was put at the centre of Nazi propaganda. Posters, magazine articles, newsreels and films contained his image. Radio was widely used to broadcast his speeches. Cheap radios were mass-produced and there were loudspeakers in the streets. Sirens announced that he was about to begin and factories stopped work. Hitler made 50 radio broadcasts in 1933, reaching an estimated 80 per cent of the German people.

The cult of Hitler was an important part of this Nazi ambition for popular support. The essence of the cult was that he was an ordinary man but set apart from all other groups and factions to represent all that the German people really felt and wanted. He was projected as a man of the people who had come to the fore to solve his nation's problems. Hitler played up to this, with an austere life-style, unmarried, being careful never to be photographed wearing glasses. He was portrayed as always kind to children and animals, and respectful of the elderly. He told an audience in 1937:

> It is a miraculous thing that, here in our country, an unknown man was able to step forth from the army of millions of German people, German workers and soldiers, to stand at the fore of the Reich and the nation.

If Hitler was popular, then that proved that his will was identical with the will of the German people and so his dictatorship was justified.

He was therefore above the law. Or rather, his own devotion to Germany, and his overwhelming popularity meant that 'constitutional law in the Third Reich is the legal formulation of the historical will of the Führer', as Nazi Justice Minister Hans Frank put it in 1938. So this meant that even the brutal, gangster-style murders of the Night of the Long Knives in June 1934 (see page 48) were justified. At least 85 people were killed without trial, 12 of them Reichstag deputies. Yet this was seen as Hitler exercising his will on behalf of the people by carrying out a necessary 'cleansing' of unruly, drunken, corrupt and violent elements.

■ Choose two words or phrases of your own or from the list provided on page 73 that you think capture the most important characteristics of Hitler's leadership based on what you have learned so far. Then briefly explain why you think each word is appropriate, using examples to support your choice.

Your words could reinforce each other or you may prefer to choose two that show contrasting aspects of Hitler's popularity.

Popularity with the people

▷ Hitler greets enthusiastic supporters in 1938 while party members hold back the crowds.

For more on the ***autobahns*** see page 86.

The laughing, cheering crowds to be seen on newsreels at the opening of ***autobahns*** (motorways), the masses of 'pilgrims' in the roads around Berchtesgaden hoping to catch a glimpse of their Führer, the people in the photo above, all seem to be genuinely enthusiastic. His appearance anywhere was an emotional experience. His arrival in Hamburg – a city where the Nazis had never done well in free elections – was recorded by Luise Solmitz, a teacher in Hamburg who was married to a Jewish ex-pilot and war hero (see also page 20):

> I shall never forget the moment when he drove past us in his brown uniform, performing the Hitler salute in his own personal way ... The enthusiasm [of the crowd] blazed up to the heavens.

Traditional religion played a large part in the life of many Germans and after 1934 the Churches were the only popular organisations left outside the Nazi Party. German Protestant Churches had always seen themselves as bastions of the nation and swastikas were soon seen in many churches. Roman Catholic leaders endorsed him too. Hitler's total opposition to atheistic Communism (which he always called 'Bolshevism') gave them common ground. The Fulda Conference of Roman Catholic bishops, in 1936 reported:

> Germany must be made militarily stronger to ensure that not only would Europe be cleansed from Bolshevism, but the entire rescued civilised world will be able to be thankful to us ... The task which this imposes upon our people and Fatherland follows as a matter of course. May our Führer, with God's help, succeed in completing this terribly difficult undertaking with unshakable determination and faithful participating of all fellow Germans.

Throughout the Nazi period many Germans distinguished between members of the Nazi Party and some of the actions of the Nazi government, and Hitler himself. Several local Nazi Party officials certainly abused their power, enriched themselves, drove big cars and commandeered desirable homes from their former Jewish owners. They were to be seen eating and drinking in expensive restaurants while the standard of living of most Germans was static. Yet Hitler remained untainted by these scandals. Most Germans took the view that 'if Hitler had known' he wouldn't have allowed these abuses.

Beyond propaganda

The cult of the leader was not created by Göbbels' propaganda: it built on some deep-rooted traditional German ideals. From long before Hitler was born, German culture had celebrated the *führerprinzip*, the principle of a leader-hero. Such a leader would arise from among the people and be self-sacrificing for the rescue of the nation. The endless debates and weaknesses of the Weimar years, outlined in Chapter 3, left many Germans eager to see the clear, firm leadership which Hitler and the Nazis promised.

Our sources for what the German people really thought pose problems for the historian. There are the reports from government, police, Party and the *Sicherheitsdienst* (SD) security services. These were confidential, and did not hide criticisms, but people knew they could get into trouble by commenting unfavourably on the Nazi government, and particularly Hitler himself. On the other hand there are the reports secretly sent from Germany to the Social Democrat Party (SPD, or SoPaDe) abroad. Naturally they were eager to latch on to any anti-Nazi murmurings. As Ian Kershaw says in *The Hitler Myth*:

> However imperfect, the historian's judgement, based on patient source criticism … and a readiness to read between the lines, must suffice.

Hitler's popularity in the years from 1933 was enhanced by what many Germans saw as real achievements. The restoration of national pride through rearmament and the re-occupation of the Rhineland in 1936 brought widespread approval. So did the decline in unemployment. The actions of the Gestapo in 'dealing with' drunks, social nuisances and outcasts, regular criminals and those seen as work-shy met with quiet agreement. In the four plebiscites held by the Nazis, (1933, 1934, 1935, 1936) they received the support of 90 per cent or more of voters. This widespread approval reached a peak in 1940 with the rapid and extraordinary military successes against Poland and most of western Europe.

■ Choose two more words or phrases of your own or from the list provided on page 73 that you think capture the most important characteristics of Hitler's leadership based on what you have learned from pages 76 to 77.

Briefly explain why you think each word is appropriate, using examples to support your choice.

Your words could reinforce each other or you may prefer to choose two that show contrasting aspects of Hitler's popularity.

Remember what the propaganda was saying: only Hitler knew what all Germans wanted, so his will was law.

Hitler's part in the government of Germany

The dictator's style

Now it's time to look at the other side of the pfennig as we look beyond Hitler's personal popularity and consider his actual involvement in policy-making and matters of state. Will the same words you have chosen still apply?

Once in power, Hitler swiftly by-passed all key features of the democratic Weimar constitution that he inherited, as you discovered in Enquiry 4. The Reichstag hardly ever met after 1934, and then only to applaud his speeches. The cabinet of ministers, which had met 72 times in 1933, was soon also made redundant: it met 4 times in 1936, 7 times in 1937, once in 1938, then never again. Local government was taken over by officials appointed from Berlin; usually the local state governor was the local Nazi Party boss, the *gauleiter*. This simply left all decision-making power in Hitler's hands. Only the civil service remained intact, willingly carrying out his decrees.

Hitler's way of working was very unusual. He liked to stay up late watching films until the small hours, so he did not start the next day until at least 10 am. He would spend the morning reading documents and reports with Hans Lammers, the Head of the Chancellery – his civil service. He might have a conversation with one or more of his ministers. Lunch was at 1 pm, or later, and Hitler was joined by whoever was around, including those ministers closest to him, but also personal servants like his chauffeur. After lunch he might continue discussing policy issues: this usually meant Hitler doing nearly all the talking. Ministers would try to get an idea of what he wanted by listening and working it out for themselves. A casual remark by Hitler would be taken as an instruction to implement a particular policy. Werner Willikens, a Nazi Food Minister, in a speech in 1934, described this as 'working towards the Führer'. Hitler himself rarely wrote out what he wanted. Ministers did not meet together to take collective decisions.

The result was chaos. Rival ministers jockeyed for power between themselves, with overlapping and competing responsibilities. Sometimes decrees contradicted each other and had to be withdrawn. You can see that access to Hitler was crucial. It was because they had this access that Göring, Göbbels, Himmler, Bormann and later Speer, Hitler's closest colleagues, were so powerful. See Insight on page 81.

■ Hitler's dictatorship was confusing and inefficient. Did this make him more powerful, or less powerful?

■ Choose two more words or phrases of your own or from the list provided on page 73 that you think capture the most important characteristics of Hitler's role in government based on what you have learned on this page. (You can choose words you selected in earlier sections if you think a theme is developing.)

Briefly explain why you think each word is appropriate, using examples to support your choice.

Your words could reinforce each other or you may prefer to choose two that show contrasting aspects of Hitler's dictatorship.

Strength and weakness

This is where you may see what was meant at the start of this enquiry when we explained that historians must choose their words carefully. In what is now rather an old debate, there was a major issue that divided historians from the 1950s to the 1980s. In the years after the war it seemed obvious that Hitler was an immensely strong dictator. The title 'master of the Third Reich' was used by historians. He was Head of State, Commander-in-Chief of the Army; he was above and outside the law: how much stronger could one man be? The accused at the Nuremberg War Trials, were eager to take this view as it enabled them to shift all blame onto the dead dictator. Historians also labelled this interpretation as 'intentionalist', meaning that everything that happened in Nazi Germany was what Hitler intended.

In the 1960s, a new generation of historians, notably Hans Mommsen, pointed out some of the features of Hitler's rule explored on the previous pages: his chaotic working style, his reluctance to make decisions, his lack of attention to detail, which resulted in power lying with leading Nazis, who built up massive personal fiefdoms, like Himmler's huge SS police empire, or the economic empire of Hermann Göring (see page 93). Germany was, in Mommsen's phrase, a polyocracy – that is, that power rested in several places. Hitler was therefore a weak dictator. Historians labelled this interpretation 'structuralist', because they said Hitler's power was limited by the structures he had to deal with in Germany – the army, the civil service, industrialists and Nazi *gauleiters*.

More recently, Ian Kershaw offered a more complex explanation. He believes that while it is true that the system was chaotic, and Hitler was lazy, erratic and hated detail, that does not mean he was weak. Hitler allowed rivalries to flourish between his minsters because, according to his beliefs, the strongest would win. This policy of 'divide and rule' ensured that he was the final authority, the source of all power, because everyone needed to get his agreement before anything could happen. It was Kershaw who picked up the phrase 'working towards the Führer' (see above) to describe how this system actually operated. However powerful other Nazi bosses, or army generals, or industrialists were, it was Hitler's vision, his ideas, which always prevailed. His overwhelming popularity confirmed and authorised this authority. There was no opposition, from individuals or groups or institutions, inside or outside the Party. Indeed, jostling with rivals for power, some leading Nazis were not so much 'working towards the Führer' as 'working past the Führer'.

With no restraint on his power, and with seeming mass support, from the late 1930s Hitler seems to have begun to believe his own propaganda and move to even more radical policies. Increasingly savage persecution of the Jews, the euthanasia policy, and the drive to war and the decision to invade the USSR, all came from Hitler's personal beliefs and obsessions.

Concluding your Enquiry

Bearing in mind all the words you have selected so far, if you had to choose between saying Hitler was a weak or a strong dictator, which would you select and why?

Choose your own single word or phrase to summarise both Hitler's popularity and his way of ruling Germany and explain why you believe it is appropriate. It may be a word you have selected already, but your explanation must show that it covers all the aspects of Hitler's dictatorship that you have considered in this Enquiry.

Insight

Making laws in the UK and in Nazi Germany

There has been criticism, in the UK and in Germany, of the fact that Nazi Germany is studied so much in schools. While it is certainly true that there are many other worthwhile history topics, and it is probably unwise to study the Nazis more than once, I think there are good reasons for regarding a study of Nazi Germany as an important part of the democratic education of every young person.

In Chapter 3 you saw how a well-intentioned fully democratic system, the Weimar Republic, was wilfully undermined and destroyed. Now you have seen the result: a dictatorship in which no German citizens had any say in laws made for their country, sometimes involving matters of their own life and death. You can read about where this led in Chapters 5, 7, 8 and 9.

The differences between how laws were made in Nazi Germany and how they are made in Britain can be seen in the two diagrams here. The contrast is stark.

Making a law in the UK today

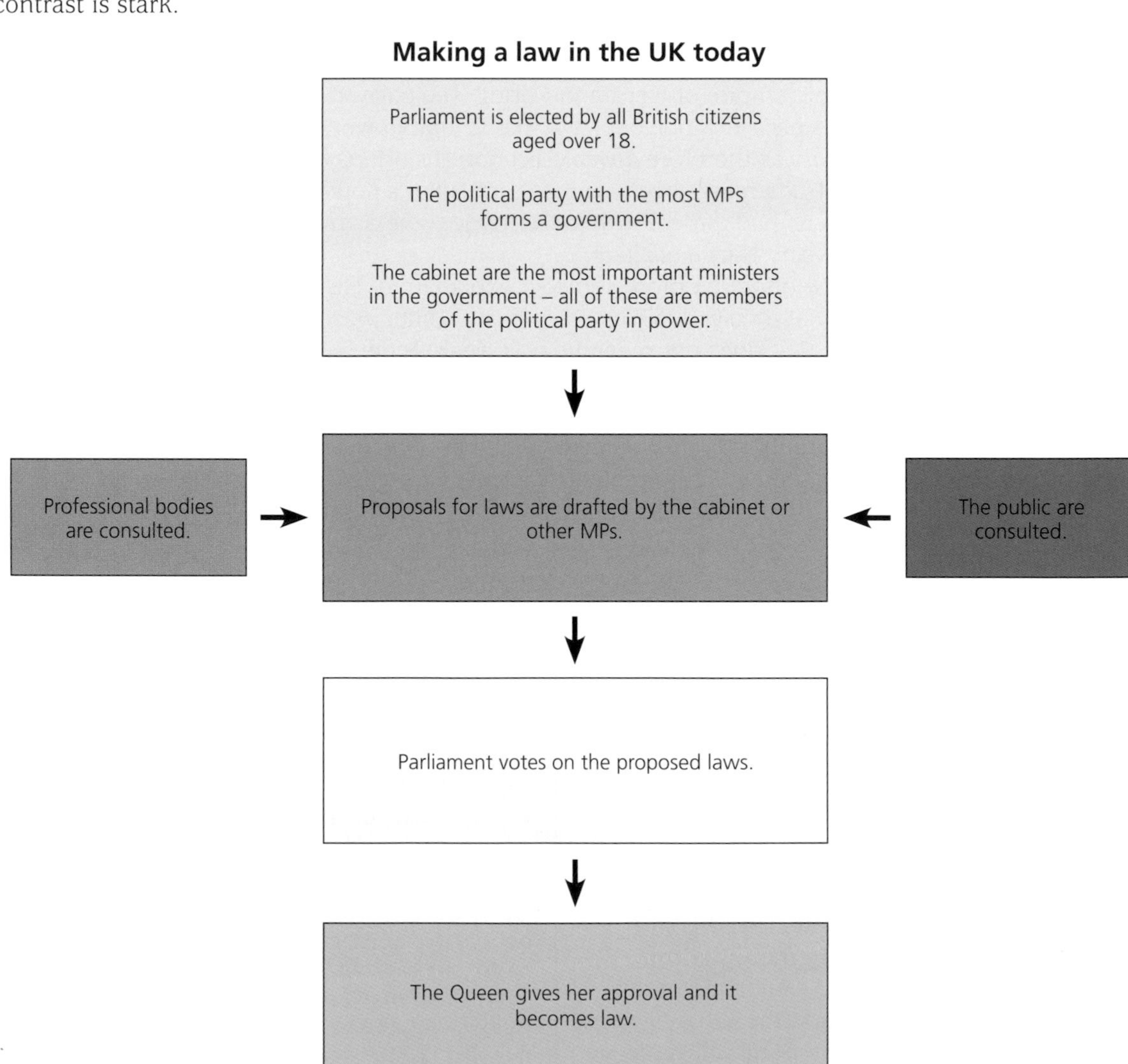

Making a law in Nazi Germany

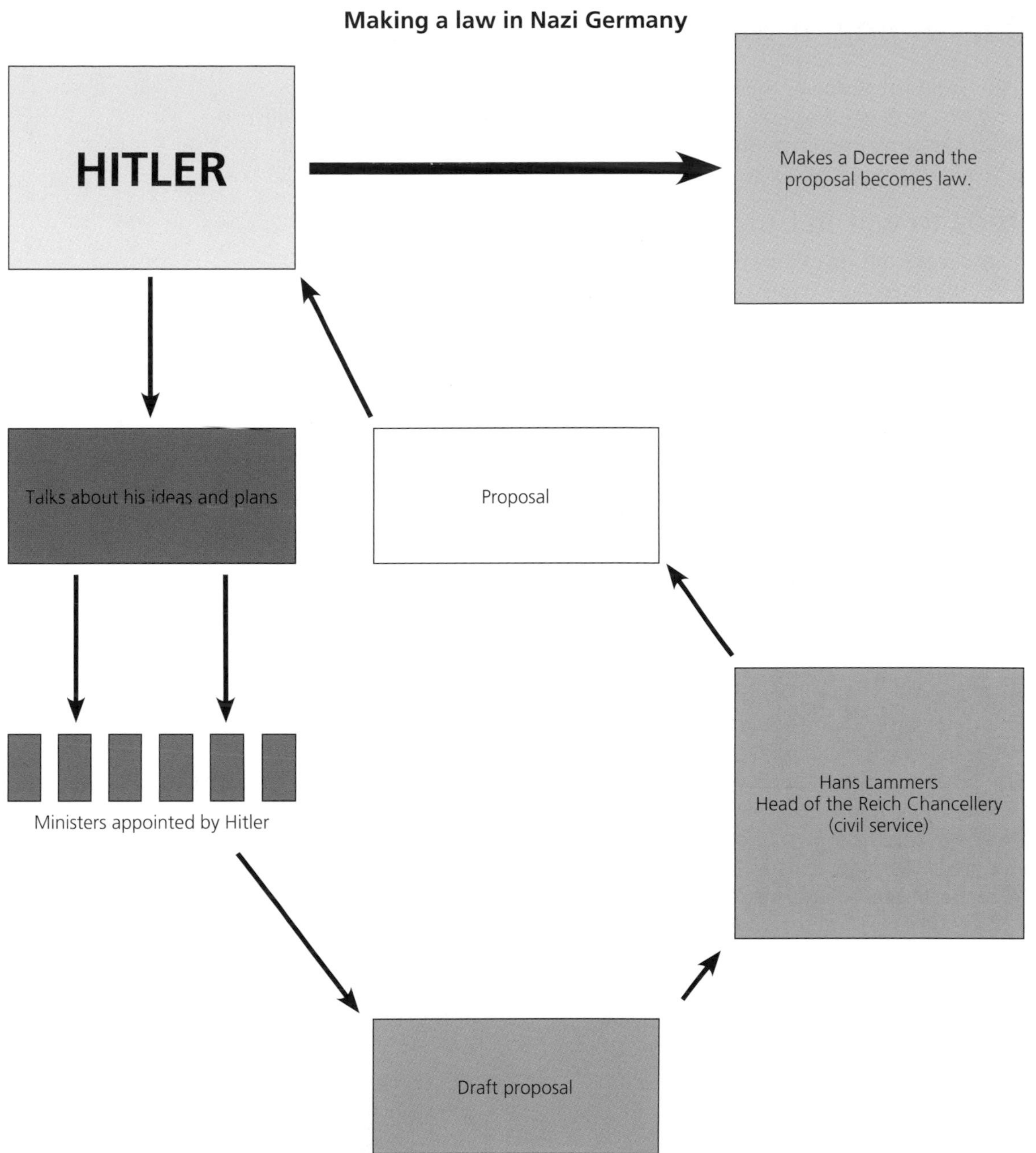

Look at the two diagrams. Explain to a partner how each one worked. Look at and compare the roles of:

- The people
- Ministers
- Ministers acting together as a collective government
- Hitler and the Queen

The coming of war

It is beyond the scope of this book to analyse exactly why the Second World War broke out or how the campaigns were fought. But the maps and notes here aim to explain three important stages that you need to grasp if the rest of this book about Nazi Germany is to make sense.

Steps to war in Europe

The outbreak of war in Europe in September 1939 came at the end of a series of aggressive acts by Germany. These began in 1935 when Hitler expanded the German army, navy and air force far beyond the limits set by the Treaty of Versailles. This went more or less unchallenged by the world's major powers. So did the re-occupation of the Rhineland in March 1936 by German troops, breaking the Versailles requirement that this border region must remain demilitarised.

By the end of that year Hitler had shown his intention to build Germany's power base in world affairs by reaching significant agreements with two military-minded states, Italy and Japan. These became known as the Axis powers. We now know that his plans to extend German territory were made abundantly plain in 1937 in a secret document known as the 'Hossbach Memorandum', but this damning evidence was only uncovered many years after the war.

For more on the Hossbach Memorandum, see page 89.

In February and March 1938, Hitler bullied Austria's government into entering a union (*Anschluss*) with Germany, yet another action expressly forbidden by the Treaty of Versailles. Once again none of the so-called great powers took action to stop him. Probably encouraged by the attitude of these powers, Hitler then provoked a prolonged crisis between April and October 1938 that ended with Germany taking the Sudetenland region from Czechoslovakia on the grounds that its German-speaking people wanted to be part of a German state. In March 1939 German forces took over the rest of Czechoslovakia. Nations such as Britain, France and the Soviet Union protested – but decided it was too late to do anything. Nor did they act when Hitler's troops occupied the Lithuanian port of Memel that same month.

Exasperated by the failure of western powers to restrain Hitler, the Soviet Union reached a startling agreement with its bitter enemy Germany. The Nazi–Soviet non-aggression Pact of August 1939 pledged that Germany and the USSR would never to go to war with each other. This was a clear sign that the USSR would not defend Poland if Germany were to invade. And it soon did.

▽ Central Europe 1938.

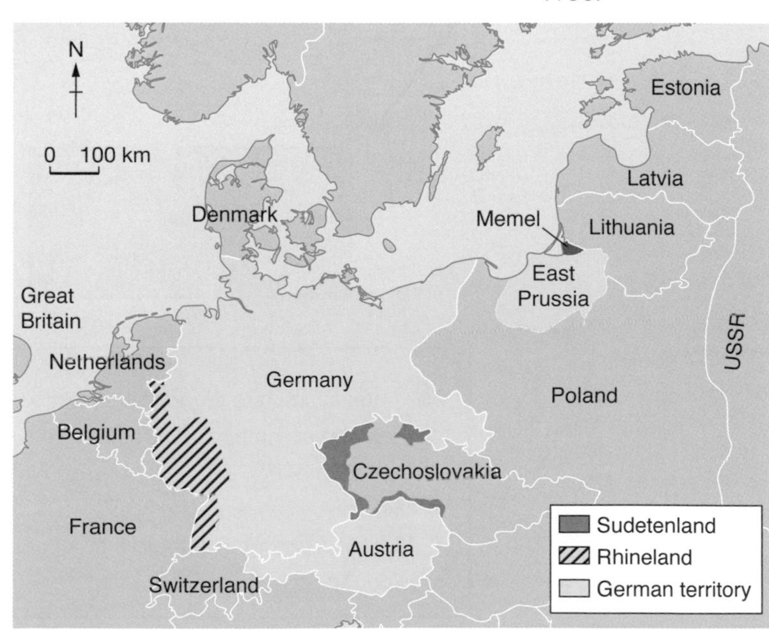

German success

From 1 September 1939 when they invaded Poland, until late 1942, Germany's armed forces swept from victory to victory. In the west, France was defeated and Britain isolated. To the east, Germany took Poland and, with her Italian allies, occupied south-east Europe. Then in June 1941 Hitler broke his treaty with Stalin and ordered a massive invasion of the Soviet Union. By September 1942 the Germans had pushed far into Russian territory but were being held at Moscow and at Stalingrad, the gateway to the vast Soviet oilfields.

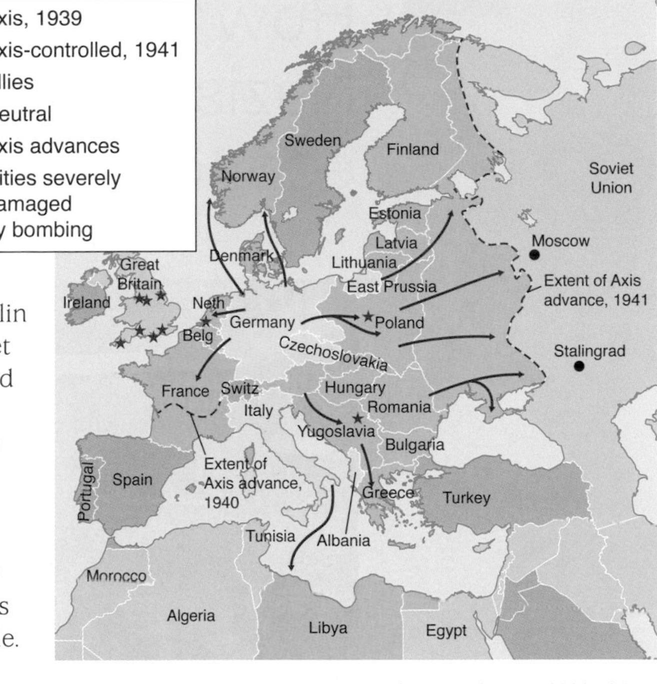

△ The Second World War in Europe 1939–41.

German defeat

In December 1941 the USA entered the war against Germany. Her wealth and the USSR's desperate resistance proved to be unbeatable. In 1942 British forces in north Africa won their first land success against the German Army. By 1944 the Soviet Red Army was forcing the Germans to retreat and was taking control, not only of its own lands, but of a host of states in eastern Europe. From June 1944 the Germans were pushed back in the west as well, following the D-Day landings of British and American forces in France. Finally, in May 1945, Germany surrendered.

▽ The Second World War in Europe and Africa 1942–45.

Impact

Beneath this rapidly told outline of the war are millions of complex human stories. Just some of these stories will emerge in your final three enquiries into three different aspects of Germany's history that were shaped by the war:

- the story of her economic development
- the story of the minorities in Germany and in the lands occupied during the war
- the story of the Nazis' defeat and why they fought for so long.

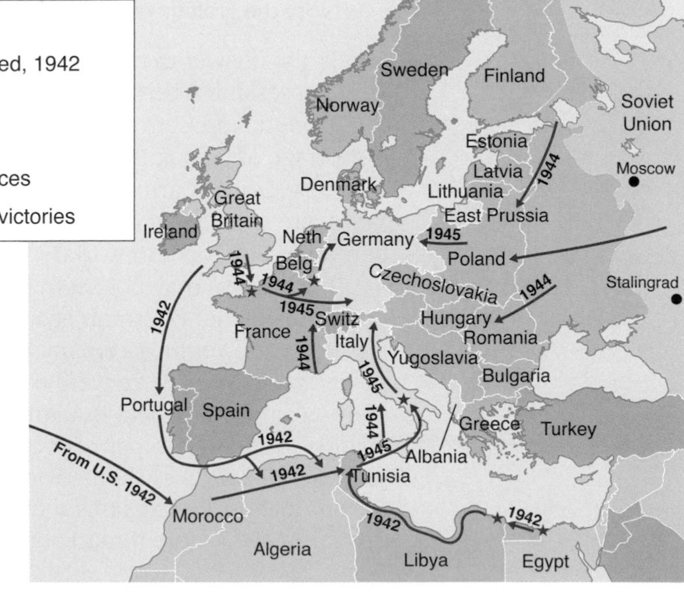

7 How successfully did the Nazis manage the German economy?

△ Unemployed people queuing at an employment office in Hanover in 1930. (Note the graffiti: WAHLT HITLER – vote for Hitler.)

Surely the answer to the question for this chapter must be that they were very successful! After all, when Hitler became Chancellor in January 1933 six million Germans were unemployed; by 1939 there was actually a shortage of labour. Furthermore, the extraordinary military conquests made by German armed forces in the first three years of the Second World War were surely only achievable with the successful industrial economy demanded by modern warfare.

This success may not seem quite so remarkable to any observer of the powerful, efficient German economy as it is today and has been for the last 50 years. Yet the Germany Hitler took over was not a great economic power at all. True, there were the massive industrial enterprises of Krupp, Siemens and IG Farben. But large parts of the economy were still very old-fashioned. Nearly 25 per cent of the population worked as peasant farmers or in handicraft workshops. Their standard of living was below average for Europeans. Perhaps this makes the Nazis' management of the German economy even more remarkable.

■ **Enquiry Focus:** How successfully did the Nazis manage the German economy?

This enquiry asks you to make a judgement about the success of the Nazis' economic management. In doing so, you will examine the roles played by some leading Nazis. You will also find out more of Hitler's own beliefs, and this means getting to grips with some very non-twenty-first century thinking. Today, management of the economy is seen to be a government's prime function. Politicians might disagree on what should be done with their nation's economy, but it is their priority. Hitler did not have the same priority. 'The economy is of secondary importance,' he insisted. You will examine what this meant in how he handled five key issues:

1. Solving the unemployment problem
2. Re-arming Germany so that the country was ready for war
3. Making Germany self-sufficient
4. Working with German industry
5. Winning a major war

As A level students, you are expected to get beyond the kind of simpler responses you might have given when you were taking GCSE. As you get deeper into a topic, you soon realise that it gets more complicated, and simple assertions are not good enough. In your last enquiry you had to show that you can sum up complex situations with a concise word or phrase. This time you face the reverse challenge: when you have learned how the Nazis dealt with each problem, you'll be given a statement that will be too general, too simplistic. Your task will be to show that you understand the complexities by adding the necessary qualifications, amendments and extra details.

When you've done that, you will make a judgement about whether you think the Nazis' economic management was successful. Make your own copy of the slide-line below to place each item where you think it should go, from 'Success for the Nazis' to 'Failure'.

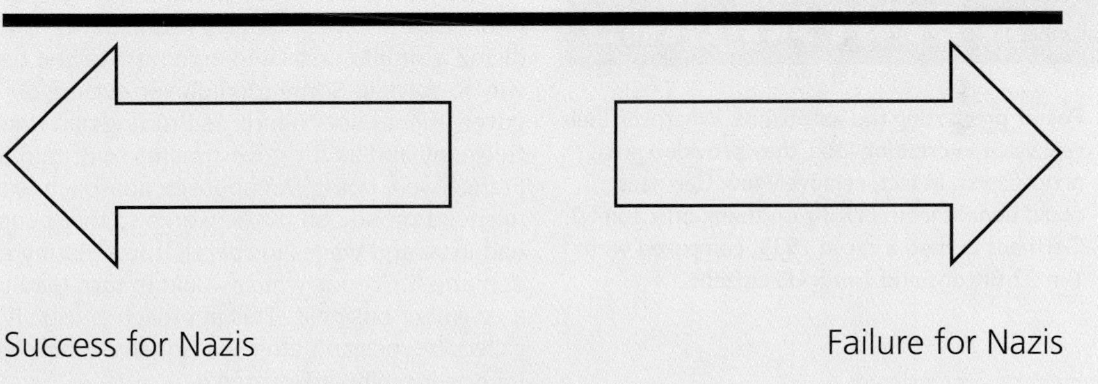

Success for Nazis

Failure for Nazis

△ Poster promoting the autobahns. Whatever their real value in creating jobs, they provided great propaganda. In fact, relatively few Germans could benefit from driving on them: only 1 in 60 Germans owned a car in 1935, compared with 1 in 22 Britons and 1 in 5 US citizens.

Key issue 1: Solving the unemployment problem

The simple answer to how the Nazis solved Germany's unemployment problems was that they put people to work building *autobahns* (motorways). Hitler loved cars, their speed, their modernity, their technology and the sweeping curves and sleek bridges of the *autobahns* built for them. He personally joined in selecting routes which revealed to best advantage the magnificent German landscape. There was also a military benefit, as the *autobahns* would enable armed forces to be moved rapidly from one German frontier to another. (There was some doubt about this, however, as the roads were probably not strong enough to take tanks.) Fritz Todt, an 'Old Nazi', was put in charge of the *autobahn* building programme. He promised it would create 600,000 jobs. (An 'Old Nazi' was someone who joined the Party in the early days of the 1920s, when it was struggling, rather than one of those who joined after 1933 in order to help their careers. Hitler always had a soft spot for Old Nazis and favoured them for top jobs.)

Germany's unemployment problem needs to be seen in context. Every country was facing a similar crisis and arguing over the best way to solve it. Some tried drastic cutting of government expenditure, as Brüning had done in Germany and as the governments of Britain and France were doing. An opposite approach was to spend money on public works so that people had jobs, and wages to spend, thus creating a demand for goods which would in turn lead to a revival of business. This approach is usually called 'Keynesian', after the British economist, JM Keynes, who advocated it.

Mefo bills were credit notes, backed by the Reichsbank but issued by a new company, *Metallurgische Forschung* (or Mefo) and payable, with interest, in five years. This method of financing also hid the growth of spending on rearmament.

So were the Nazis Keynesians? Hardly. Government spending on job creation was only adopted as Nazi policy for the 1932 elections to support Hitler's promise to solve unemployment. The 500 million Reichsmarks the Nazi government spent on job creation schemes had in fact been set aside by Schleicher during his brief period as Chancellor. Nevertheless, the Nazis added 1000 million Reichsmarks in the 'Reinhardt Programme' in June 1933 and another 500 million Reichsmarks in September. This money took the form of credits which could be taken up by private industry for public works such as road construction, repairs and town improvement. Cautious at first, Hitler appointed Hjalmar Schacht, a non-Nazi, as Economics Minister, who devised a clever method of funding this government expenditure through **Mefo bills**.

Unemployment certainly declined rapidly, from 6 million in early 1933, to 2.2 million in 1935, to less than a million by 1937. Can the Nazis take credit for this?

Some of the decline in unemployment was simply due to various ways of removing people from the figures. One of the most dramatic was the **Marriage Loans Scheme** of June 1933. The main condition of the Marriage Loan, which could be up to 1000 Reichsmarks, was that the woman had to stop working until it was paid off. Paying off the loan took about eight years, on average, during which the women were not recorded as 'unemployed'.

For more on the **Marriage Loans Scheme**, see page 62.

More workers were taken off the unemployed list through having to do Labour Service. This was compulsory work for all unemployed males aged 18 to 24 for six months, usually in unskilled physical work, such as agriculture or building airfields or barracks. On the other hand, part-time farmworkers, usually women who helped out on the farm at important times, were now registered as employed, further improving the figures by lowering the percentage of unemployed. The government was also helped by the fact that the numbers of young people coming into the labour market from 1933 was relatively small: they were those born during the First World War, a much-reduced cohort.

The historian Adam Tooze describes the 'hidden unemployed' and calculates that there were still about 4 million out of work in 1935. Nor did the work creation schemes deliver the promised numbers of jobs. Only about 1000 were working on autobahns in 1933, only 38,000 by 1935. Unemployment fell by 2.6 million by the end of 1934. Of this reduction, 289,000 in 1933 and 1,079,000 in 1934, or only 38 per cent, was due to action taken by the government. The Keynesian theory, that wages from new jobs would lead to business recovery hardly applied: pay and conditions on job creation schemes were poor. Well into 1935 consumer spending remained below the 1929 level. Two other factors were far more influential in getting Germany back to work: the world was gradually pulling out of depression anyway, trade was slowly increasing, and with it jobs were returning. And Hitler had embarked on a massive rearmament programme, as we shall soon see.

■ Here is a simple assertion:

'The dramatic reduction in unemployment in Germany after 1933 was a Nazi economic miracle.'

Write your own amended version of this statement about the fall in unemployment so as to reveal the complications of the real picture.

On your own copy of the Success/Failure line shown on page 85, indicate your judgement about Key issue 1: Solving the unemployment problem.

Key issue 2: Re-arming Germany

△ U-boats being built at Bremen. This photo gives an idea of the scale of rearmament, in this case of submarines, a type of warship which Germany was not allowed to have according to the Treaty of Versailles.

Only nine days after becoming Chancellor, on 8 February 1933, Hitler told his cabinet:

> The next five years in Germany must be devoted to the rearmament of the German people ... Germany's position in the world will be decisively conditioned by the position of Germany's armed forces.

At this stage, and speaking to a cabinet which contained only two other Nazis, he does not talk of war. Rearmament itself, the total rejection of the restrictions imposed on Germany by the Treaty of Versailles, was one of the policies which the Nazis shared with the other nationalist parties in what was then a coalition government. As he explains, rearmament was to do with Germany's 'position in the world' – its pride, so dear to the old élites. He also had to bear in mind Germany's weakness and vulnerability at that time. In his own mind, and to his followers, however, war was inevitable – indeed necessary.

Conscription, announced in 1933, began in 1935. Following their six months' Labour Service, all males had to serve for a year in the armed services, raised to two years in 1936. The Treaty of Versailles had limited the German armed forces to 100,000. By 1939 there were 750,000 in the army, 333,000 in the air force and 80,000 in the navy.

In May 1933, Hitler appointed Göring, the ex-First World War fighter pilot, as head of the new Reich Aviation Ministry. He planned massive expansion of the *Luftwaffe* (air force), even though this was specifically barred by the Treaty of Versailles: 2000 fighter planes, 2000 bombers, 700 dive-bombers, and over 1000 other aeroplanes. Hitler expected to fight a land war against Poland and Russia, but was persuaded by Admiral Raeder to plan a huge expansion of the German navy as well (the figures in brackets are the limits imposed by the Treaty of Versailles): 8 battleships (6), 3 aircraft-carriers (none), 8 cruisers (6), 48 destroyers (12), 72 submarines (none).

Iron, steel and weapons factories expanded fast to meet the orders. In November 1933, the navy, for example, placed orders worth 41 million Reichsmarks for guns and 70 million Reichsmarks for ships. Some of this military expansion was carried out in secret. Planes were built, and pilots trained, in the USSR; Krupps began to build 'agricultural engines' – which were in fact tanks, also specifically barred by the Treaty.

By 1936 Hitler could be more explicit about his aims. The Four Year Plan, to be managed by Göring, was specifically 'to prepare for war within four years'. In November 1937, Hitler told a meeting of the chiefs of the armed forces (in the Hossbach Memorandum, so-called from the name of the officer who took the minutes):

> The aim of German foreign policy is to secure and preserve the racial stock and to enlarge it. It is therefore a question of space …
>
> Germany's problems could only be solved by the use of force.

Hitler had written that this would be 'necessary' in *Mein Kampf*, in 1924 (see pages 18–19).

By the end of the 1930s, spending on armaments was swallowing up a huge percentage of Germany's **GNP**, as this table shows:

The Gross National Product (**GNP**) is the total value of all the wealth created by a state each year.

1933	1.5%
1934	7.8%
1936	15.7%
1938	21.0%

△ Percentage of German GNP spent on arms. In 1938 the UK was spending 8 per cent of its GNP on armaments, the USA 1 per cent.

Such rapid expansion of the armaments industry put several strains and stresses on the economy.

- Big orders for armaments provided thousands of jobs: only 13 million Germans had jobs in 1933, but by 1938 19 million were in work. With conscription as well, unemployment had virtually been eliminated by then – in fact, there was a shortage of workers. Women were enticed to work in factories and in 1936 women who had received a Marriage Loan were allowed to work. In 1933, 1.2 million women were working; by 1938 this had risen to 1.8 million. But the shortage of labour still held production back.
- By 1938, 25 per cent of Germany's entire steel output was needed for the army. Other areas of production, such as consumer goods, were kept short of supplies. The standard of living of the German people failed to rise despite Hitler's promises back in 1933.
- Raw materials had to be imported from abroad, but imports had to be paid for. By 1938, Germany's trade deficit was 9.8 billion Reichsmarks and the national debt had risen to 31 billion Reichsmarks. Schacht was deeply opposed to this level of debt so Hitler forced him out of his position as Economics Minister. Hitler's view was simply:

> However well balanced the general pattern of a nation's life ought to be, there must at particular times be certain disturbances of the balance at the expense of other less vital tasks. If we do not succeed in bringing the German army as rapidly as possible to the rank of premier army in the world ... then Germany will be lost!

- The demand for raw materials, particularly iron, steel, rubber, glass and chemicals far outstripped the ability of German industry to supply them. (See also Key issue 3, below.)

Few of the targets for military strength listed above were actually met. For example, aircraft production actually fell in 1938, owing to lack of steel. Germany started the Second World War with less than 5000 aircraft of all types. German forces in 1939–41 achieved spectacular success with *blitzkrieg* (lightning war) tactics. However, given their limitations, Germany was only really able to wage this kind of rapid war rather than sustain a long drawn out conflict. This issue is explored further in Key issue 5.

■ Here is your next simple assertion:

'The Nazi government successfully prepared Germany for war by 1939.'

Write your own amended version of this statement so as to reveal the complications of the real picture.

On your own copy of the Success/Failure line shown on page 85, indicate your judgement about Key issue 2: Re-arming Germany so that the country was ready for war.

Key issue 3: Making Germany self-sufficient

As we saw on pages 18–19, Hitler was deeply affected by Germany's defeat in 1918. Among other reasons, he blamed Germany's dependence on foreign imports of food and raw materials, which were blockaded during the war. The result was widespread hunger and the loss of morale which led to defeat. The answer, as he laid out at length in *Mein Kampf*, was to make Germany self-sufficient. That way the country would be able to fight a long war, if necessary. His name for this self-sufficiency was Autarky.

As soon as he came to power Hitler set about trying to create Autarky.

1. **Food** Through the National Food Corporation, targets were set for every stage of food production from farmers to shopkeepers. Many peasants resented these controls, but the policy did have limited success. By 1939 Germany was self-sufficient in bread, potatoes and sugar. However, 15 per cent of the country's food was still being imported, such as butter, meat and vegetables. Rationing began well before the war, in 1937, and was extended in 1938 to cover coffee and fruit.
2. **Industrial raw materials** Home production of iron, steel and coal were all increased. But here the policy of Autarky clashed with the enormous drive to re-arm. So great was the need for iron ore that imports rose, from 4.5 million tonnes in 1933 to 21 million tonnes in 1938, despite the increase in home production. Important products which Germany could not produce at all were rubber and oil, so chemists were put to work to find and make artificial alternatives. An artificial rubber, called *buna*, was invented and manufactured by IG Farben. However, it never met more than five per cent of Germany's needs.

It was obvious that Autarky was not working. In 1937 Hitler abandoned it, but not the wider aim of protecting Germany's economy in the event of war. Importers were encouraged to develop suppliers in south-east Europe, an area which Hitler expected would soon be under his control.

■ Here is your next simple assertion:

'The Nazi government failed to make Germany self-sufficient in food and raw materials.'

Write your own amended version of this statement so as to reveal the complications of the real picture.

On your own copy of the Success/Failure line shown on page 85, indicate your judgement about Key issue 3: Making Germany self-sufficient.

Key issue 4: Working with German industry

What kind of relationship were the Nazis going to develop with German industry?

The signs were confusing: after all, the Nazi Party's full name was the National Socialist German Workers Party. Were the Nazis going to take over the entire economy in the name of the workers, as Stalin was doing in the USSR at the same time? But those ideas belonged to the Nazi past. From the mid-1920s Hitler had cultivated industrialists, emphasising his hostility to Communists. It was business magnates like the newspaper baron Alfred Hugenberg who had propelled Hitler to the Chancellorship in January 1933, not so much as their favourite choice, but as the 'least worst' of the alternatives that Weimar could come up with.

See differing historians' interpretations of economic policy, on pages 8–9.

Indeed, both at the time and since, Marxist historians have painted Hitler as the tool of the capitalist bosses. Historians in the DDR (East Germany) pointed to his suppression of trade unions as early as May 1933; they contrasted the low wages paid to workers with the massive profits industrialists made from rearmament contracts (see Key issue 2). The rearmament programme certainly cemented close relationships between the Party, the Army and the armaments manufacturers in the years from 1933 to 1936.

In the west, the argument has been over which was dominant: economics or politics. Most historians, even those on the left, were clear that political considerations under the Nazis took priority over economic concerns. Richard Overy, for example, wrote in 1982: 'Industry was subordinate to the interests of the party.' Alan Milward wrote: 'However sympathetic to the business world, and however dependent on it, the Nazi government had its own interests which it was prepared to pursue.' This was increasingly the case after 1936, when Hitler summed up his intentions for the Four Year Plan very starkly:

> 1 The German Army must be operational within four years.
> 2 The German economy must be fit for war within four years.

Hitler showed the same approach to industry and the economy that he took with the military. Difficulties could be overcome with enough 'determination' and 'ruthlessness'. Economic or technical problems were 'excuses'. He was impatient and lectured industrialists:

> There is no point in the endless repetition of the fact that we lack foodstuffs and raw materials; what matters is the taking of those measures that can bring about a final solution for the future.
>
> It is not a matter of discussing whether we are to wait any longer ... It is not the job of ... government to rack ... its brains over methods of production.

If private industry couldn't deliver, then he would get rid of them. The problems of labour shortages and lack of raw materials could only be solved by war, by seizing the raw material reserves and by enslaving the peoples of conquered lands. It was simply the job of German industry to fulfil the second of the two aims listed above.

◁ Himmler touring the IG Farben *buna* plant at Auschwitz, which used slave labour from the concentration and death camps (see pages 120–121), 1942.

More recently, historians have rejected the simple opposition of 'politics first' or 'economics first' in favour of an understanding of the close working relationship between party, army and industry. IG Farben, for instance, had seen their profits rise from 74 million Reichsmarks in 1933 to 240 million Reichsmarks by 1939, almost entirely thanks to government contracts. Their technicians worked with Nazi government officials on the Four Year Plan. By 1943 they owned 334 factories across the expanded territory of the Third Reich. The company helped to build concentration and death camps, used slave labour from them and supplied the gas used to kill Jews. A private company had taken on, not just the business, but the ideology, of the Nazis.

However, the Nazi government was increasingly prepared to go into business on its own account. In 1936 ***Reichswerke Hermann Göring*** was asked to organise the construction of three huge new iron and steel plants. Two-thirds of the funds were provided by government. When private companies objected to the one-third of the funding they had to provide for what was obviously going to be a competitor, Göring threatened to have them shot for sabotage. *Reichswerke Hermann Göring* went on to take over most Austrian steelworks after the Anschluss of 1938, and the Skoda factory in Prague after Czechoslovakia was seized in 1939. Other businesses and factories were increasingly taken over by Nazi Party leaders – by 1939, for example, virtually all Germany's newspaper, magazine and publishing businesses were in Party hands.

Reichswerke Hermann Göring was a state-owned industrial complex involved in mining, iron and steel. Set up in 1937, it was run by Hermann Göring.

■ Here is your next simple assertion:

'The Nazis worked side by side with German industry.'

Write your own amended version of this statement so as to reveal the complications of the real picture.

On your own copy of the Success/Failure line shown on page 85, indicate your judgement about Key issue 4: Working with German industry.

Key issue 5: Winning a major war

Historians argue over the reasons why Hitler triggered the start of the Second World War by invading Poland in September 1939. Was the timing of this decision driven by economic factors – the shortages of labour and raw materials were never going to improve unless Germany could seize resources and workers by making conquests in the east? Or was it driven by diplomacy? After the German seizure of Bohemia in March, 1939, Britain and France were preparing for war, with explicit US support, so he may have thought it was better to strike early.

From your reading of this chapter so far, which interpretation seems to you the more likely?

By 1944 the RAF had 8300 aeroplanes and the Soviet air force 17,000.

Whatever the motivation, the ambitious targets of the 1936 Four Year Plan were nowhere near met. And nor could they be. The *Luftwaffe* was supposed to have 21,000 aircraft by 1940; in fact it only had 5000. The target was unrealistic in many ways, not least because such a huge air force would require twice the world's supply of fuel.

▷ **625,000 horses were used to transport supplies for the German Army during the invasion of the USSR in 1941. Here a gun-crew are struggling to ford a river.**

Four Year Plans for the navy fell short in the same way, and were just as unrealistic. The fact was that the mix of state and private business in the rearmament programme was chaotic. Inflated claims were not supported by effective planning. Iron and steel production, essential for all forms of armaments, depended on coal, which had to be transported from the mines by rail. But the German railway system had been neglected in favour of more prestigious projects. In 1939, drastic reductions in targets had to be made. The projected target of 61,000 machine-guns, for example, was reduced to 13,000.

The *Wehrmacht* (army) stood at 750,000 men in 1939, but they were short of equipment; many were living in tents as there was not enough barrack accommodation. Rapid victories against Poland in 1939 and western Europe in 1940 were achieved through air superiority and by dramatic *blitzkrieg* tactics with fast-moving Panzer tanks. But two-thirds of the army moved on foot, with horse transport to supply them.

The New Order

As you can see from the map at the top of page 83, by the end of 1941 the Nazis controlled most of Europe, with a population of 290 million, greater than that of the USA. Some in Germany talked of a 'New Order', a continent united in a working partnership. But the Nazi attitude towards their conquests was simply to plunder them. From ordinary soldiers grabbing food and drink from French peasants, to Göring raiding the art treasures of Europe for his own collection, the approach was the same. In October 1940 Göbbels made no secret of Nazi aspirations: 'When this war is over we want to be the masters of Europe'.

From France alone Germany seized over 300,000 rifles, 5000 artillery pieces, nearly 4 million shells and over 2000 tanks, as well as thousands of locomotives and trucks to prop up the inadequate German railway system. Raw materials, especially vital metals, and large supplies of petrol were seized. The French calculated that by the end of the war 7.7 billion Reichsmarks worth of goods had been seized and not paid for. Holland, Belgium, Denmark, Norway and Poland suffered in the same way. In addition, the conquered states had to pay 'occupation costs', which for France amounted to 20 million Reichsmarks per day.

While German companies took over factories in many places, local industries were also required to meet production targets to supply the German war effort. They never did. With low morale and poor nutrition, this is not surprising. Occupied countries were never even invited to become part of a New Order.

Forced labour

Conquest was also the Nazis 'answer' to the labour shortage. By 1943, the army was losing 60,000 men a month on the eastern front. These men could not be replaced by taking Germans from factories and farms. Instead, they had to be replaced, by 'volunteers', forced labour or prisoners of war (PoWs). By 1942 there were 4.7 million foreign workers in Germany. They were a common sight in every city: in Munich there were 120 PoW camps and 286 hostels for foreign workers. The BMW plant alone employed 16,600 foreign workers. Of all foreign workers 58 per cent were women and the government complained that too many were simply being employed as house servants.

As for the treatment of foreign workers, Himmler's famous, and chilling, declaration says it all:

> Whether 10,000 Russian women collapse with exhaustion in the construction of an anti-tank ditch for Germany, only interests me insofar as the ditch gets dug.

None of the foreign workers were treated well, although racist attitudes prevailed and those from western Europe fared better than those from the east. Food was poor, housing inadequate and medical attention minimal. Foreign workers were not allowed to fraternise with local people, but were locked in their hostels at night. When sexual liaisons with Germans developed, the foreigner, if male was executed, if female and became pregnant, her baby was taken away and killed.

Death rates were high: of 8.4 million foreigners who worked in Germany at some point during the war, only 7.9 million were alive in 1945; it was worse for PoWs: of 4.5 million taken, only 3.4 million were alive in 1945.

The Speer 'Miracle'

Albert Speer was Hitler's favourite architect; Hitler fancied himself as a bit of an architect and they spent many happy hours together planning grandiose schemes for Nazi cities after the war. (See Insight, pages 122–123). In February 1942, with no clear end to the war in sight, Hitler appointed him Minister for Armaments. He had no business experience, but set about applying business methods to the chaotic German armaments industry. He later claimed that within 6 months 'total productivity in armaments increased by 59.6 per cent. After two and half years (from 1942–44), in spite of heavy bombing, we had raised our entire armaments production' by over 50 per cent. Monthly aeroplane production in 1944 rose from 1323 in February to 3538 in September.

He did this by bringing 6000 business managers into his ministry. They concentrated on standardisation and productivity. The number of types of lorry being made was cut from 151 to 23; the different types of aircraft from 42 to 5. Suppliers were put on standard, fixed-price contracts.

■ In 1946 the US economist JK Galbraith asserted that Germany should have won the war. Do you think the evidence in this section supports that conclusion?

It was all in vain. After the surrender of the remnants of the German Army at Stalingrad the war was lost. Hitler was determined to fight on to the bitter end (see Chapter 9), and Speer gave him the means to do so. Millions more died as result. Germany's increases in production could not get near the feats of the mighty arsenals of the USA and USSR. For example, in 1943 Germany produced 166,000 machine guns; combined allied production was 1,100,000; in 1944 Germany produced 6000 tanks; the USSR 19,000 and the USA 28,000.

Speer seems to have charmed the judges at Nuremberg by accepting some blame and claiming ignorance of the Holocaust (he was lying). He received a twenty-year sentence and wrote his memoirs. Historians have looked carefully at Speer's claims and have cast doubts on many of them. He chose low starting points for production figures, so that his claims appeared greater. Most of the new managerial innovations he claimed to have brought in were introduced by his predecessor. He claimed credit for production increases in areas he was not in fact in charge of. Many of the factories which achieved high rates of aircraft production did so by violent coercive methods. A 72-hour working week was the norm, with overtime on top. Managers who failed to meet targets were court-martialled. Thousands of slave labourers from concentration camps were brought in and worked, literally, to death.

Allied bombing raids played havoc with armaments production by 1944. The disruption of the railways was particularly disastrous, see, for example, the photograph opposite. By then, Speer turned to new 'wonder weapons' which would swing the war Germany's way again: a new U-boat, the Mark XXI, a jet fighter, the Me 262, and the V1 and V2 rockets. The first two were never operational and the rockets, while causing many civilian deaths, did nothing to halt the Allied advance. The rockets were produced in tunnels at Mittelbau; most of the workforce were from the concentration camps at Dachau and Oranienburg. The workers slept inside the tunnels, deprived of fresh water and sanitation. Those not working to the satisfaction of the managers were hung from the rafters. Speer saw a factory littered with corpses when he visited it in December 1944.

Here is your final simple assertion:

'Nazi Germany was never going to be able to fight a long war.'

Write your own amended version of this statement so as to reveal the complications of the real picture.

On your own copy of the Success/Failure line shown on page 85, indicate your judgement about Key issue 5: Winning a major war.

◁ A destroyed German railway from Allied bombs during the Second World War.

Concluding your Enquiry

Until now, you have been taking simplistic assertions and amending them to reveal the complexities. This is where you must use what you have learned to devise your own general (but NOT simplistic) answer to this enquiry question, How successfully did the Nazis manage the German economy?

1 Look again at your Success/Failure line, which should now have five points marked on it.
2 Use these decisions to arrive at your own, general, 'headline' answer to the question.
3 Now list ten key points you would use from this enquiry to show that you can defend your generalisation with supporting evidence. You may well find the ideas for these in the extra details you added to each of the generalisations you have challenged up to this point.

Insight

The musician, the monument and the mayor

△ Statue of Felix Mendelssohn in Leipzig. The name on the statue is the full name by which Mendelssohn was baptised. It ends with his mother's surname 'Bartholdy'. This surname had been adopted by his mother's Jewish family, from a property they owned, in an effort to break away from their Jewish roots.

This statue shows the figure of a German musical genius of his day: Felix Mendelssohn. He was born in 1809 and by the age of twelve he had written twelve symphonies that the great poet Goethe declared to be better than the early works of Mozart. In his twenties, Mendelssohn became what we might today call an international superstar. He performed his music to adoring audiences in Britain, France, the Netherlands and of course in his homeland – Germany. The piece you are most likely to recognise from his work is popularly known as the *Wedding March*, taken from his *Midsummer Night's Dream*.

Then in 1847, at the age of just 38, in his adopted home city of Leipzig, Felix Mendelssohn died. Some years later, in 1892, a large bronze statue of the composer was erected in the city. But this is not it.

The story of Mendelssohn's statue reveals some of the absurdities and complexities around Nazi policies on race, in the years just before those same policies led to the programmes of mass murder that you will explore in your next enquiry. For, although Mendelssohn had been baptised into the Lutheran Church, and had lived as a practising Christian, he was born a Jew. Under Nazi policies, baptism could not change his race. It was also impossible to hide Mendelssohn's Jewish background because he was the grandson of a well-known Jewish philosopher Moses Mendelssohn and because, just three years after his death, another great German composer, Richard Wagner, had famously written a pamphlet denouncing Mendelssohn and other Jewish composers as an evil influence on German music. By the 1930s Wagner was celebrated by the Nazis as the greatest of all musicians and his anti-Semitic views had become central to Nazi cultural policy.

In 1933, when Hitler came to power, Josef Göbbels established the *Reichsmusikkammer* (State Music Institute). It declared what music was to be celebrated as an example of the superior Aryan race and what was to be banned as un-German and corrupting. Beethoven, Bach, Mozart (even though he was Austrian) and, of course, Wagner were examples of high German culture. But jazz and swing were deemed '*Negermusik*' (negro music) and therefore to be regarded as a degenerate influence on the young. Popular Jewish American composers such as George Gershwin and Irving Berlin were banned from German radio. And even the world-famous Mendelssohn could not escape criticism.

Following Wagner's attacks in the 1840s, many of Mendelssohn's original manuscripts had been gathered and stored in the basement of the Berlin State Library where eventually, in the mid-1930s, they were smuggled out of Germany by his musical supporters and taken to Poland. The statue erected in Leipzig in 1892 presented a greater difficulty. In 1936, the deputy mayor of Leipzig, Rudolf Haake, was a Nazi. The mayor, Carl Goerdeler, was certainly no lover of Jews, but he was not a Nazi and resisted their extreme racist policies. He even hoped somewhat naïvely that he and others could restrain Hitler so that Germany could truly benefit from his rule. The mayor and his deputy fell out over what should be done with Mendelssohn's statue. Haake insisted that it should be torn down but Goerdeler refused. Their struggle continued for months, until, in the autumn of 1936, Goerdeler went away on a trip to Finland, having first gained the personal promise of Hitler and Göbbels that nothing would happen to the statue in his absence. He returned to find that the statue had been taken down on the orders of Haake. The bitter row continued for months but by spring 1937, Goerdeler could see that his authority as mayor had been fatally undermined and he resigned his post.

From that time, Goerdeler worked in opposition to the Nazis. He was in secret contact with politicians across Europe and in the USA and, once war broke out, he developed his links with highly placed Germans who, like him, believed Hitler was endangering their homeland. By 1944 his opposition had taken him to the point where he had been chosen as the man to take over from Hitler as Chancellor had the 20 July plot to assassinate the Führer succeeded. When it failed, the secret service raided his hotel room and found hundreds of incriminating documents including the speech he would have broadcast to the German people had he become Chancellor.

Goerdeler was executed on 2 February 1945.

And the statue? The original was never found. It had probably been melted down. But in 2008, ready for the bicentenary celebrations of Mendelssohn's birth, a new statue, shown opposite, was erected in Leipzig city centre. On its base is written:

Edles nur kunde die Sprache der Tone.
(The language of music proclaims only the noble.)

8 In what ways were Jews treated differently from other victims of Nazism?

Hitler's vision for the German people, as we saw in Chapter 5, was a People's Community. To be part of this community, and benefit from it, you had to:

1 Support the Nazi government without question.

   This meant giving the Führer your total loyalty and obedience and demonstrating your support by using the Nazi salute and greeting (*Heil Hitler*!) on all possible occasions.

2 Work hard and uncomplainingly at whatever tasks the state required.

3 Be of pure German blood (whatever this racist term means! See the Social Darwinism box on page 102).

Those who would not, or could not, fit into this national community were outsiders and all became victims of the Nazis, suffering persecution and death. Several of those outsider groups ended up in concentration camps and had to wear the badges shown.

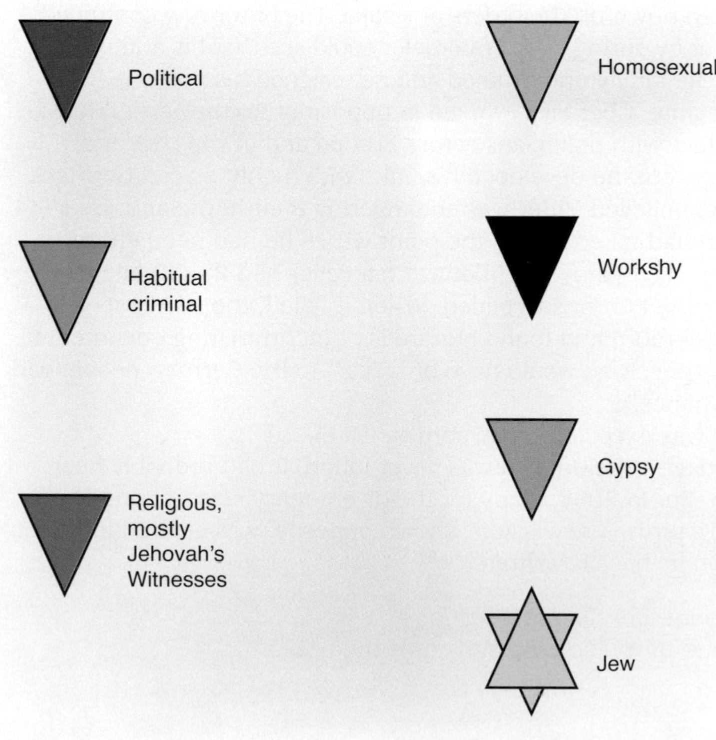

▷ Badges worn by different groups in the Nazis' concentration camps.

Enquiry Focus: In what ways were Jews treated differently from other victims of Nazism?

In this enquiry you will learn about different groups who became victims because they fell outside the Nazis' view of who could be a member of the new German community. The groups you will study are shown in the table below. In each case you need to decide why the people in that group became victims of the Nazis. What was it about their beliefs, lifestyle or ethnicity which put them outside the People's Community?

You will also need to record how they were treated and whether this changed over the twelve years of the Third Reich. At the end of the enquiry you will use your notes to put together your responses:

- What changes were there over time in which groups became victims of the Nazis and in the ways they were treated?
- We will then be in a position to consider the main question: Whether (and if so, how) the Nazis' treatment of the Jews was different and distinctive from all the other eight groups you will have considered.

	Why they were persecuted	**Dates of persecution**	**How they were persecuted and whether this changed over time**	**How and why their persecution changed**
Socialists and Communists				
Asocials				
Jehovah's Witnesses				
Homosexuals				
Gypsies				
African heritage				
The disabled				
Poles, Russians and Russian prisoners of war				
Jews				

Social Darwinism, racism and 'blood'

In the late nineteenth century some writers developed a distorted version of Darwin's explanation of evolution, published in 1859. Darwin described natural selection as the survival of the fittest forms of animal or plant life; Social Darwinists applied this to the survival of the strongest 'races'. They believed that some 'races' were superior to others, carrying certain characteristics in their blood. It was therefore very important to keep the blood 'pure'. By natural selection through conflict, the superior race would triumph over inferior races and eliminate or rule over them. The English writer Houston Chamberlain particularly described the conflict between the Germanic (or 'Aryan') and the Jewish races. Some German writers insisted that 'the Germanic race has been selected to dominate the earth'.

Hitler met up with and responded to these ideas in Vienna before the First World War. He repeated them in *Mein Kampf*, (see pages 18–19), and they provided him with his driving force, right to the end.

Political enemies

The Nazis' bitter political enemies were the Social Democrats in the SPD and the Communists in the KPD. For years they had both been the targets of brownshirt violence on the streets and at their meetings.

To the Nazis, the SPD was tainted as the party of the Weimar Republic. It was the main architect of the Weimar constitution, it was in power for most of the Weimar years and so stood for all the Nazis hated about multi-party democracy. The Nazis also hated the SPD for being the party whose representatives signed the Treaty of Versailles. With more than one million members and links with the powerful trade union movement, the SPD was a force to be reckoned with. Its leadership was always at pains to maintain its role as a respectable, law-abiding, non-revolutionary party, but with its own paramilitary organisation, the Reichsbanner.

The Nazis hated the KPD for its internationalism, its close links with the USSR and its belief in equality of all people. It was much smaller than the SPD, with 180,000 members. But it was tightly-knit and well organised to defend itself against persecution. The Communist paramilitary organisation, the Red Front-Fighters League (*Rotfrontkämpferbund*) had fought many street battles with the brownshirts. In one of these, in Berlin in 1930, the young Nazi Horst Wessel was killed, becoming a hero celebrated in the most famous Nazi marching song, the *Horst Wessel Lied*.

Together, the SPD and the KPD had won 221 seats in the Reichstag in the November 1932 elections – more than the Nazis' 196. But they would never work together. Memories of 1919, when the Social Democrat government had turned to the right-wing Freikorps to crush the Communist revolutionaries and murder their leaders, were too strong. The SPD poster from 1932 opposite, portrays the Communists as almost as much of a threat as the Nazis.

For more on this period, see Chapter 4, especially pages 38–39 and pages 43–44.

Within six months of the Nazis coming to power in January 1933 both these parties were broken. Göring had been appointed Prussian Minister of the Interior, so was in charge of half the police in Germany. He appointed the brownshirts as auxilliary police, giving them licence to storm through towns and cities, attacking Communists, Social Democrats and trade unionists. Party offices were broken into and set on fire, their meetings blocked. Following the Reichstag fire at the end of February 1933, the entire Communist leadership was arrested, beaten and held captive. By May 1933, 100,000 Communists and Social Democrats were under arrest; at least 600 had been killed. This uninhibited, licensed violence intimidated many of those not actually taken.

In addition to those who were simply locked in cellars of Nazi Party buildings, 70 concentration camps were hurriedly erected to hold the prisoners. By then, the storm of mass arrests of Communists and Social Democrats had abated. One-third of those arrested were freed by July 1933 and most of the rest over the next twelve months; by the end of 1934, only 3000 political prisoners were in custody. Most concentration camps had been closed, leaving only four: Dachau, Sachsenhausen, Buchenwald and Lichtenburg (the women's camp).

At the same time, known Social Democrat or Communist Party members were excluded from all government jobs, which included all teachers, judges and civil servants. They were banned from working for newspapers or radio. Many fled into exile. Those who were killed were not all victims of Nazi gangs. The courts were ready to hand down death sentences, rising each year from 64 in 1933 to 117 in 1938. Among the first to be executed – by hand-wielded axe – were four young Communists in Hamburg, watched by brownshirts, SS and other Nazis. In 1934 Hitler set up 'People's Courts' (see page 46), with two professional judges sitting with three Nazis: the whole process of the law had rapidly become entirely politicised. In the years 1934–39, 3400 Communists and Social Democrats were tried and executed or given six-year prison sentences.

△ SPD poster from 1932. The text says;

These are the enemies of democracy!

Away with them!

So vote List 1

Socialdemocrat!

'Asocials'

All kinds of people fell into the category of those labelled 'asocial' or 'undesirables'. This included tramps, vagrants, alcoholics, habitual criminals, prostitutes, beggars and those people who were simply eccentric. In addition, with almost full employment by the later 1930s, the Nazi government came down on those who would not, or could not, hold down a regular job; they were labelled 'workshy'. The German 'race' had to be purged of such people.

As the Nazi government became more secure in the latter years of the 1930s, it became more radical. In March 1937, police drew up lists of 'habitual criminals'; 2000 were arrested and sent straight to concentration camps, however trivial their offences. From December 1937 anyone who the regime defined as 'asocial' could be arrested and the numbers in the camps, which had dwindled since 1934, began to rise again. Political prisoners were soon outnumbered: 4600 of the 8000 prisoners at Buchenwald were those categorised as 'workshy'. Himmler said they were there to learn 'obedience, hard work, honesty, good order, discipline, cleanliness, sobriety, truthfulness, self-sacrifice and love of the Fatherland'.

■ Complete the first two rows of your copy of the table shown on page 101, recording the treatment of Socialists, Communists and asocials.

Jehovah's Witnesses, homosexuals and gypsies

Jehovah's Witnesses

There were 30,000 members in Germany of the Christian-based religious sect of US origin known as Jehovah's Witnesses. They refused to do national service, to swear to obey the Führer, to give the Hitler salute, and had as little as possible to do with everyone outside their own tightly-knit membership.

Even though they posed no threat, the Nazis could not tolerate them. Many were arrested, imprisoned and sent to concentration camps. All attempts to break their faith failed; they quietly withstood beatings and even welcomed martyrdom. By 1945, 10,000 Jehovah's Witnesses had been imprisoned, 2000 of them in concentration camps where nearly 1000 died.

Homosexuals

In the liberated atmosphere of the Weimar years, Berlin and other cities developed a flourishing gay culture, which the Nazis hated as degenerate, unmanly and an offence against the propagation of the German race. Himmler in particular was deeply homophobic and Hitler described homosexuality as: 'infectious and as dangerous as the plague'. The SA leader Ernst Röhm's homosexuality was widely known; this enabled Hitler to defend the Night of the Long Knives, June 1934 (see page 48) as a purge of undesirable elements.

Lesbians were sometimes arrested as part of the treatment of 'asocials' but on the whole were left alone.

In 1937 the law was tightened up and increasing numbers of men were arrested for homosexuality. Altogether 50,000 homosexuals were arrested during the Third Reich, half of them in the years 1937–39. As soon as their prison sentence was over many were sent straight to concentration camps. They had to wear the pink triangle and suffered unending victimisation from guards and **kapos**. Some camp commandants, like Höss at Sachsenhausen, believed that 'hard work and strict discipline' would 'cure' them. The death rate for homosexuals in the camps was 50 per cent.

As with most other victims described in this chapter, persecution was stepped up during the war years. Homosexuals in camps were often 'persuaded' to undergo castration. Himmler ordered that SS members convicted of homosexuality would be 'shot while trying to escape'.

Prisoners trusted to help run the concentration camps were known as **kapos**. They were often crueller than the guards.

Gypsies

Gypsies failed to fit into the Nazis' People's Community in so many ways that you are going to have difficulty when it comes to filling in the enquiry box at the end of this section!

Originally from India (not Egypt, as their English name suggests), Gypsies arrived in Europe in around 1000 BC or perhaps earlier. Two 'tribes' emerged over the centuries: the Sinti, mainly living in Germany and northern Europe, and the Roma, in southern Europe and the Balkans. There were about 35,000 gypsies in Germany and Austria in the 1930s (figures are hard to establish as Gypsies tended to avoid state controls such as birth and death registration). Laws restricting the movement and settlement of gypsies had already been passed in several states under Weimar and when the Nazis came to power, Gypsies soon became their victims. The attack on 'asocials' from 1933 led to many arrests of Gypsies, on the grounds that they were social misfits, no better than beggars or petty criminals and had no fixed residence. Under the 'Law for the Prevention of Hereditary Diseases of Offspring', 1933, some were forcibly sterilised on the grounds that their asocial behaviour was hereditary.

The Nuremberg Laws, 1935 (see below), grouped them with Jews and people of African heritage as having 'alien blood'. The restriction on mixed marriages applied to Gypsies, so it became necessary to register exactly who was, and was not, of Gypsy 'blood'. In the crazy pseudo-science of race, Gypsies were undeniably Aryan, speaking an Aryan language – Romani. The Department of Racial Hygiene was set up in 1938 to try to register all Gypsies. It was decided that 'pure' Gypsies (about 10 per cent) should be protected, while the rest were of 'mixed blood' and had 'hereditary criminal tendencies'. Gypsy children who could not speak German were classified as 'feeble-minded', taken from their parents and sterilised.

These distinctions only mattered to keen race scientists. In 1936 all gypsies in Berlin were rounded up and placed on a small field at Marzahn. Six hundred Gypsies were forced to live there, with three water taps and two toilets. Soon disease was rife and many died. Some lived there for years, awaiting deportation. Similar actions were taken in other cities.

As we have seen, the war changed everything for the worse. Gypsies in Poland and Russia were rounded up and shot. Gypsies from Germany began to be deported to newly-conquered territories in the east from 1939 onwards. One group was just tipped out of their train in the middle of empty countryside and left to starve. Even Gypsies serving in the German Army were picked out and deported. Large scale deportations of gypsies to death camps began in 1942, mainly to Auschwitz. In August 1944, 2897 gypsies were put to death there in one night. With few reliable records of the original Gypsy population it is hard to tell how many were killed: estimates vary from 220,000 to half a million.

Treatment of Gypsies in the countries conquered by the Nazis varied a great deal, but many local pro-Nazis carried out their own killings of Roma – at least 36,000 in Romania and slightly more in Croatia.

■ Complete the next three rows of your copy of the table shown on page 101, recording the treatment of Jehovah's Witnesses, homosexuals and Gypsies.

Concentration camps

Conditions in the first concentration camps were chaotic and brutal, but in June 1933 Himmler appointed Theodor Eicke as Commandant at Dachau concentration camp near Munich. The system he introduced there became the pattern on which all the later camps were based. He brought in strict discipline for the guards, good weapons and a proper uniform – including the 'death's head' badge. Prisoners were subject to very strict discipline and treated by the guards with utter contempt. The rules gave the guards a sense of superiority, and a feeling of security against being tried in the courts for any of their actions. In 1935 Himmler set up the special division of the SS to run the camps.

Punishments were given at the whim of the guards, including beatings with a cane, a whip or a strap, solitary confinement in tiny hutches or being hung up for hours by the wrists. Guards were encouraged to hate and humiliate the inmates, or relieve their boredom and isolation by tormenting them.

By 1939 the numbers in the concentration camps had risen to 21,000 and new camps had been opened. All inmates endured a brutal regime. Work was now a major part of camp life. After roll-call at 4 am, prisoners laboured at hard physical tasks such as road-mending or quarrying, with another long roll-call at the end of the day. Death rates were extremely high, from savage punishments and shootings, from being worked to exhaustion and, in winter, from hypothermia, but also from diseases, such as typhus, which flourished in the over-crowded and insanitary conditions among people weakened by excessive labour and poor diet.

The system of triangle badges (see page 100) was introduced to distinguish the different types of prisoner in the camps. Dividing the prisoners in this way made them easier to control. Much of the daily supervision of prisoners was in the hands of 'kapos' – trusted prisoners. They were mostly habitual criminals and exercised cruel control over all other prisoners.

African heritage Germans and the disabled

Germans of African heritage

There were about 500–600 black Germans of African heritage. The story of their origins, put about by Nazi propaganda, was that they were 'Rhineland bastards' – the result of rapes of German women by black African soldiers in the French Army during the occupation of the Rhineland in 1923–24. In fact, some were the result of consensual relationships with French soldiers, but many were the children of colonists from the German African Empire who had married African women. From 1937, the teenage children of these mixed relationships, both boys and girls, were forcibly sterilised.

The disabled

Ideas of racial purity and racial health were widely held around the world in the early twentieth century and made sense to Hitler, obsessed as he was with 'race'. As early as July 1933 the Nazis passed the Law for the Prevention of Hereditarily Diseased Offspring. A range of disabilities and conditions were listed which were said to be hereditary, from physical conditions, such as blindness, deafness and epilepsy, to psychological conditions, such as schizophrenia, depression and what was called 'feeble-mindedness'. This also included social ailments such as alcoholism. Doctors were obliged to report the names of any of their patients who might fall into any of these categories. They were encouraged to look for 'signs' of hereditary degeneracy, such as the shape of the ear-lobes, or finger-nails. Cases were then investigated by special Hereditary Health Courts, consisting of two doctors and a lawyer. Those people who were thought to pose a risk of passing on their condition were **sterilised**. (Some of these conditions were, in certain genetic circumstances, hereditary and some certainly were not.) It became a huge business, with 84,500 cases heard in 1934, 90 per cent of whom were sterilised. Altogether, nearly 400,000 people were dealt with in this way, mostly before 1939. Physical disability made up only 1 per cent of cases, especially as the war drew near and anyone who could work was needed.

Do not think that this kind of crazy but cruel policy existed only in Nazi Germany. In the USA, 28 states had similar **sterilisation** laws and so did Switzerland, Denmark, Norway and Sweden – the latter until 1975.

The euthanasia programme

As Nazism became more radical towards the end of the 1930s, their leaders discussed, but dared not introduce, the obvious next step: killing off those who had, as they put it: 'a life unworthy of life', in other words – a euthanasia programme. To Hitler, these people were not only contributing nothing to their country, but enfeebling the German race as it steeled itself for war. As far back as 1935 he had said to the Reich Doctors' Leader that he would bring in euthanasia '... when the whole world is gazing at acts of war and the value of human life in any case weighs less in the balance'. Preparations were made to kill up to 70,000 adults.

The war changed everything. As we shall see, Poles suffered mass killings as soon as German forces invaded. These included the inmates of Polish psychiatric hospitals, who were taken out and shot. In late 1939, a whole ward of patients was put in a sealed room and gassed with carbon monoxide – the first of the Nazis' victims to be put to death in this way. Himmler came to watch.

But what of those in Germany? In October 1939 – but with the date changed to 1 September 1939 in order to link it with the outbreak of war – Hitler decreed that incurably ill patients should be given 'a merciful death'. At first this was applied to children. Doctors were paid to report all cases they knew of a wide range of disabilities, including Down's syndrome, cerebral palsy, limb deformities and 'idiocy'. These cases were reviewed, the children taken from their parents and put in special hospital wards. There they were slowly starved to death, or given overdoses of a sedative. Some 5000 children were murdered in this way.

Then, in 1940 attention turned to adults. Gas chambers for killing adult patients by carbon monoxide gas poisoning were built. The organisation to carry out the programme, called Action T4, was set up under an SS officer, Viktor Brack. Medical officials worked alongside Nazis. Patients were taken by bus to one of the gas chambers and killed in batches of fifteen or twenty. When they were all dead, orderlies opened the sealed doors, untangled the bodies, ripped out any gold teeth they had and took them to the incinerator. Relatives received letters giving a fake cause of death; some even received urns with the supposed ashes of their loved one. Around 80,000 people were murdered in this way.

But it was impossible to keep the euthanasia programme secret. Relatives grew suspicious; locals noticed a link between the arrival of the buses and the smoke from the incinerator chimney; medical staff realised what was happening. Some patients did too; a nurse who called 'see you again' to a patient was told: 'We won't be seeing each other again; I know what lies before me with this Hitler Law'. About half the psychiatric hospitals were run by church organisations, and some clerics began to speak out. The toughest stand was taken by Cardinal Galen, Roman Catholic Bishop of Münster. In a series of sermons in July and August 1941, printed and circulated in his diocese and then picked up and read over the BBC, he told the world what was happening, and that it was wrong. He argued that people cannot be put to death because they were not productive. If so:

> then fundamentally the way is open to the murder of all unproductive people, of the incurably ill, … then the murder of all of us when we become old and weak.

The government dared not persecute Galen because of his world-wide reputation; the euthanasia campaign was halted in August 1941. The Action T4 organisation was re-directed to use its methods on other victims (see below). It has to be said, however, that Galen had little to say about the treatment of Gypsies and Jews.

■ Complete the next three rows of your copy of the table shown on page 101, recording the treatment of Germans of African heritage and the disabled.

Poles, Russians and Russian prisoners of war

The German conquest of Poland from September 1939, and then of large parts of western Russia from June 1941, brought millions more people under Nazi rule. To Hitler and leading Nazis, including most generals, this was not an ordinary war. To the race-obsessed Nazis, Poles and Russians belonged to the inferior 'Slav' race, so this was a racial war. Hitler described it as 'a hard ethnic struggle which will not permit any legal restrictions. The methods will not be compatible with our normal principles'. Under the 'normal principles' of war, civilians should not be harmed by armed forces and prisoners of war should be treated humanely and given medical care if they need it. Neither of these principles was observed.

As we shall see, German invading armies particularly sought out and killed Jews, but from the first days of the invasion of Poland, civilians, including the elderly, women and children, were also rounded up and shot in large numbers. As early as 8 September, **Heydrich** said: 'We want to protect the little people, but the aristocrats, Poles and Jews must be killed.' Educated Poles, such as teachers and priests, found themselves in particular danger as Hitler's intention was to reduce the country to a mere, dependent 'reservoir of labour' with a low standard of living. Vicious reprisals took place for the tiniest incident. A smashed window of the police station at Obluze, for example, led to the arrest of 50 local schoolboys. No one would own up; the SS ordered their parents to beat the boys and when the parents refused, the SS beat them with rifle butts, then shot ten of them. By the end of 1939, 65,000 Poles and Polish Jews had been murdered and ruthless killings went on throughout the years of German occupation.

Reinhard **Heydrich** (1904–42) was one of the key figures in the Holocaust. He chaired the Wannsee Conference (see page 119). He was assassinated near Prague in 1942.

The invasion of Russia was conducted with the same attitudes, and brought the same behaviour. In March 1941, three months before the invasion, Field Marshall von Brauchitsch instructed his troops that they:

> ... must be clear that the conflict is being fought between one race and another, and proceed with necessary vigour.

General Hoepner's marching orders in May 1941, stated:

> The war against Russia ... is the old struggle of the Germans against the Slavs ... the defence against Jewish Bolshevism ... and as a consequence must be carried out with unprecedented harshness.

'Vigour' and 'harshness' were relatively mild words to describe what followed.

The German Army's rapid advance in 1941 was accompanied by the mass shooting and rape of civilians and the looting and the burning of villages. People living in towns and cities unfortunate enough to be in the path of the invasion suffered terribly. The cities of Minsk and Kursk were reduced to rubble by bombing and shelling, their citizens deliberately starved. In some areas the Germans were initially welcomed by people who had little affection for Stalin's government, a sentiment that could have been built on. Instead, their experience of the German invaders led many Russians to join partisan groups carrying out acts of sabotage behind German lines. These were followed up by savage German reprisals against local civilians. The anger stirred up by the invaders' behaviour became a desire for revenge which was to be terribly carried out only four years later (see Chapter 9).

The treatment of Russian soldiers broke all rules of war. The Red Army included political commissars (Communist Party members) alongside their commanders. If captured, they were shot on sight. So rapid was the German advance, and so unprepared and disorganised was the Red Army at first, that thousands of prisoners were taken. Many of these ordinary soldiers were simply shot when they surrendered. Those who became prisoners of war might have preferred such an end.

In October 1941, a Polish doctor saw a column of 15,000 Russian prisoners of war pass through his town:

> They looked like skeletons, just shadows of human beings ... men were falling in the street, the stronger ones holding up the others. They looked like starved animals. They were fighting for scraps of apples in the gutter, not paying any attention to the Germans who would beat them with rubber truncheons. Some crossed themselves and knelt, begging for food. Soldiers beat them without mercy. They beat not only prisoners but people who tried to give them some food.

Field Marshall von Reichenau ordered his men to shoot prisoners who collapsed. Many Russian prisoners of war were transported by train in open trucks. In November 1941, 1000 out of a trainload of 5000 PoWs froze to death. In one prisoner of war camp in Poland only 3000 were left in February 1942 out of an original number of 80,000 after a winter of starvation, trigger-happy guards and diseases such as typhus. Cannibalism took place on a large scale. In some places, thousands of prisoners of war were simply penned in on the open plain and left to starve to death. Their howls could be heard for miles. Three hundred thousand Russian prisoners of war had died by the end of 1941.

■ Complete the next row of your copy of the table shown on page 101, recording the treatment of Poles, Russians and Russian prisoners of war.

As the Nazis recognised their labour shortage problems, Soviet prisoners of war were sent to work in slave labour camps. However, their physical state from the way they were treated was such that large numbers continued to die. According to German records, 5.7 million Russians were taken prisoner during the war; 3.3 million of them died (probably an under-estimate). This death rate of 58 per cent compares with a 2 per cent death rate for British, French and other prisoners of war.

Jews

You have now found out about many different groups of people who, in different ways, at different times and for different reasons, became victims of the Nazis. Now is the time to examine the ways the Nazis persecuted the Jews during their twelve years of rule. Remember that your big enquiry question is: In what ways were Jews treated differently from other victims of Nazism? Think about the following questions as you work your way through pages 111–121:

- Were they persecuted for different reasons?
- Were they persecuted on a different timescale?
- Is the only difference a matter of numbers? At least 6 million Jews were killed by the Nazis. This is far more than any other group of Nazi victims. Why were so many killed?
- In what other ways were the Jews treated differently from other victims of the Nazis?

You will find that we have included some tasks that focus on **turning points** to help you think about how the treatment of Jews changed over time.

Who were the Jews of Germany?

There were 523,000 Jews in Germany when Hitler became Chancellor in 1933. This was about 1 per cent of the population, so they were a tiny minority in what was a strongly Christian country. Indeed, their distinctiveness was dwindling fast: by 1930 around a third of all Jews were marrying non-Jews. As this suggests, Jews were well-integrated into German society. They had built their lives in Germany; 72,000 Jews died for their country in the First World War. They tended to live in the big cities – nearly one-third of them in Berlin – and to be strongly represented in certain professions such as law, medicine and teaching. Many were also in business, often as shopkeepers, most visibly as owners of the newest type of shop – department stores.

As you read this section of the chapter on the persecution of the Jews, record the ways in which the Jews were treated differently even from the other victims of the Nazis you have found out about already.

How strong was anti-Semitism?

There had always been an anti-Semitic element in Christianity, blaming the Jews for killing Christ. However, anti-Semitism was given a secular, pseudo-scientific thrust by the arguments of Social Darwinists (see page 102). Their emphasis on conflict between the races also gave twentieth-century anti-Semitism an edge of violence. These views could be encountered on the fringes of politics in many countries, but a third element entered German anti-Semitism after 1918: blaming Jews for the defeat in war (the 'stab in the back') and for the humiliating terms of the **Treaty of Versailles**. On the right-wing, too, Jews were blamed for the rise of Communism. Indeed, Hitler's *Mein Kampf* uses the terms 'Jew' and 'Bolshevik' together: 'Jewish-Bolshevism'. Scapegoating Jews for all Germany's ills after 1918 was common politics for parties on the right, including the Nazis. 'It's all

For more on the 'stab in the back' and the **Treaty of Versailles** see pages 13 and 15.

the fault of the Jews!' was a popular chant in the beer halls where Hitler was making his name in the early 1920s.

It was all nonsense, of course. Jewish people were not responsible for the German defeat in 1918; one of the Weimar politicians who signed the Treaty of Versailles was Jewish, but the others were not; some **Bolsheviks** (but not Lenin) and some German Communists were Jews, but most were not; most German Jews supported democratic parties of the centre right or centre left, and so on. But in the crisis-laden Weimar years anti-Semitism became part of the orthodoxy of right-wing parties and of some of those who supported them in the army and the civil service. The Nazi Party attracted support for several reasons, only one of which was its overt anti-Semitism. During the crucial election campaigns of 1930–33 Nazi speakers were encouraged to talk up their anti-Semitism if they thought the audience were receptive, but to play it down if not. Julius Streicher's (see page 74) rabidly anti-Semitic journal *Der Stürmer* (*The Stormer*), with its caricatures and obviously made up stories of sexually predatory Jews and ritual murders, repulsed many Germans.

The Russian Social Democrat Party split in 1903 and one part, the **Bolsheviks**, led by Lenin, carried out the October Revolution in 1917. The Bolshevik Party changed its name to the Communist Party in 1918.

How did the Jews lose their civil rights?

Many textbooks use a well-known photograph of SA men outside a Jewish-owned shop daubed with anti-Semitic slogans. This boycott took place in April 1933 with official support, and was widely reported in the foreign press, but was called off after only a few days. As we saw in Chapter 5, Hitler and the Nazis wanted to set up a popular dictatorship, with the support of the mass of the German people. Virulently anti-Semitic as Hitler was, he knew that most Germans did not share his extreme views. Indeed, in many towns local people showed their disapproval of the SA thugs outside Jewish-owned shops and some deliberately went ahead and used the shops. The Nazis were moving quite cautiously at first, unsure what the German people would stand for in the way of overt discrimination. Other campaigns dealt with in this chapter, for example against those classed as 'asocial', were closely watched to see what they could get away with without losing public support.

That is not to say that Jews were left alone. SA gangs regularly smashed up synagogues and Jewish business premises. Jews were beaten up in the street. By June 1933, 40 Jews had been killed by Nazi violence and by the end of that year, 37,000 Jews had left the country.

Another approach to implementing anti-Semitic policies was used in 1933: the law. With a compliant Reichstag after the March 1933 elections, the Civil Service Act (see page 42) was passed in April. This banned Jews from working for the state, and was wider than it sounds, because teachers in schools and universities, judges, railway and post office workers as well as government officials were all state employees. President Hindenburg insisted that the law was modified to exclude Jewish war veterans and those appointed by the Kaiser.

No anti-Semitic legislation was passed in 1934, but speeches by leading Nazis in 1935 increasingly demonised Jews. The Nazis had got away with their attacks on asocials, political enemies, the disabled and homosexuals, and felt they were secure enough to ignore criticism from abroad. Streicher

Turning points

As you read the next ten pages you will see that the persecution of the Jews in Germany and then in Europe proceeded relentlessly, but erratically.

What were the turning points, the moments when the Nazis' persecution of the Jews suddenly changed?

Four turning points will be identified as you read on. In each case:

- Decide whether you agree that it is a turning point.
- Analyse what makes this a turning point.
- Add any other moments which you consider to be turning points.

proclaimed 'We do what we want with Jews in Germany!' The drip-drip of propaganda, through speeches, radio broadcasts, classroom indoctrination and a totally controlled media, was slowly building up a greater acceptance of anti-Semitism. As a Social Democrat in Bavaria reported:

> The persecution of Jews is not meeting with any active support from the population. But on the other hand it is not completely failing to make an impression. Unnoticed, racial propaganda is leaving its traces. People are losing their impartiality towards the Jews ...

△ Sign saying 'Jews not welcome' in Behringersdorf (a village near Nuremberg)

Some towns and villages, hotels and restaurants under the control of Nazis or Nazi sympathisers were announcing on banners and badges that they were *Judenfrei* ('Jew-free'), or that Jews were not welcome.

In September 1935 Hitler summoned Reichstag members to Nuremberg for the last day of the annual Party rally to inform them that 'Jewish provocations' had made it necessary to pass three new laws. Göring spelt out the detail of these **Nuremberg Laws**, saying that they were necessary 'to ensure that this purity of the race can never again be made sick or filled with rottenness'.

- The Law for the Protection of German Blood and German Honour forbade marriages or sexual relations between Jews and 'Aryans'.
- The Reich Citizenship Law declared that 'only those of German blood could be citizens of Germany', so Jews could no longer be citizens of their country.
- The Law for the protection of the Genetic Health of the German people meant that all couples had to be medically examined before being allowed to marry to ensure that they were genuine Aryans and physically fit to propagate the German race.

But who exactly, in a country of many mixed marriages, the offspring of mixed marriages, and Jews who had converted to Christianity, was a Jew? The Government tried to define a Jew as someone with three Jewish grandparents. But what, then, was the status of someone with two, or one, Jewish grandparent? Family historians had a boom in business as people sought to prove their status and acquire a piece of paper called a Declaration of German Blood. In the case of mixed marriages, status depended on whether there were children, and if so, in which religious faith they were being brought up. Non-Jewish wives of Jews came under pressure, sometimes even offered bribes, to divorce their husbands, but most refused, some very indignantly. It was all, of course, a legal minefield, with hundreds of cases going to the courts each year. The effect of these laws was to define Jews in racial terms, rather than as a religious or social group. Many could see that it was all just crazy racist nonsense, but for many it was soon to be a matter of life and death.

Turning point: the Nuremberg Laws, 1935

Do the Nuremberg Laws mark a turning point in the persecution of Jews? If so, in what ways?

How were Jewish businesses persecuted?

German Jews were deeply-rooted in the economic life of the country, running all kinds of businesses from huge department stores and banks to little local shops. Their treatment is described by the British historian Richard Evans as: 'A vast campaign of plunder with few parallels in modern history'.

Immediately they came to power in 1933, the Nazis began an unrelenting attack on Jewish-owned businesses. SA gangs picketed Jewish-owned shops and smashed their windows, but much more effective was a continuing drive to force individual Jews out of their own businesses.

Jewish-owned businesses were discriminated against: marriage loan tokens could not be spent in Jewish stores; Nazi Party contracts for uniforms and supplies – especially jackboots – went to non-Jewish firms. Jewish companies faced demands for 'unpaid back taxes' and faked confessions of fraud leading to massive fines. Jews sold up their businesses to non-Jews in a process called 'Aryanisation'. In the early 1930s they usually got a fair price, but later were forced to sell at prices far below their real value. Many were bullied or cheated. For example, the Jewish owner of a small shop in Fürstenwalde, having been beaten down on its real value, was eventually handed the money. Two Gestapo men then arrived and confiscated the bundle of notes. The former owner dared not complain.

Nazis often benefited personally from these transactions, getting hold of successful shops and businesses on the cheap. Jews were driven off the boards of banks, insurance companies and businesses and then from all employment in those companies. Foreign companies operating in Germany, like Ford (US) and Geigy (Swiss) fell in with this policy. Banks did very well out of Aryanisation, charging 2 per cent commission on all the transactions. Jews who wanted to emigrate had to pay tax on capital taken out of the country. The rate reflected the increase in the level of persecution: in 1932 it was 20 per cent, in 1935 it went up to 68 per cent, in 1936 to 81 per cent and in 1938 to 90 per cent.

In 1933 Jews were operating 50,000 shops in Germany; by 1938, they had just 9000. And the pace increased: in February 1938 there were 1610 Jewish tradesmen in Munich; by October that year there were just 666. 1938 was a turning point.

In what ways was 1938 a turning point?

Pogrom is a Russian word meaning an organised assault on a group of people. The most violently anti-Semitic regime in the early twentieth century was Tsarist Russia. The word therefore came to be used for violent attacks on Jewish communities.

It is hard to leave your home, the place where you and your family and friends have lived all your lives. Although 37,000 Jews emigrated after the **pogroms** of 1933, the numbers leaving dwindled in the next few years: 21,000 in 1935, 25,000 in 1936 and 23,000 in 1937. Most emigrants, about 70 per cent, stayed in Europe (understandably but tragically, as it turned out), although 52,000 had settled in Palestine by 1939. After the 1935 Nuremberg Laws there was no further anti-Semitic legislation for a while. In 1936 signs discriminating against Jews were taken down in order to give a good impression to visitors from abroad who came to the Berlin Olympics. Many of the remaining Jews probably thought that the Nazis had calmed down: 'the soup is not eaten as hot as it's cooked', as the saying went. They were wrong.

The remaining Jews in Germany faced a fresh onslaught of persecution in 1938. Jewish doctors, dentists and lawyers were forbidden to have Aryan patients or clients; Aryanisation of businesses drove almost all Jews out of commerce; all Jewish-held property and assets had to be registered, opening them up to increased taxation. In August, all Jews had to have their identity cards stamped with a 'J' and the recognisably Jewish names of 'Israel' or 'Sara' added to their own.

In March 1938 Austria was annexed to Germany in the *Anschluss*. All the anti-Semitic measures German Jews had suffered over five years were immediately enforced on Austria's 200,000 Jews. They were banned from their professions, had their property and businesses confiscated, their homes broken into and looted. Austrian Nazis attacked and humiliated Jews in the streets, making them scrub the walls and clean toilets with their bare hands. By mid-1939, 50 per cent of Austrian Jews had been forced by threats and violence to emigrate.

Taking their cue from Austria, pressure on German Jews to emigrate mounted. Particular attention was paid to the 50,000 Polish Jews living in Germany. In October 18,000 were rounded up by police, and, with little or no preparation, put on sealed trains to the Polish border. The Poles refused to accept them, leaving them in no-man's land for several days.

One couple who suffered in this way were the parents of seventeen-year-old Herschel Grynszpan, who was living in Paris. Blazing with anger, he got a gun, went to the German Embassy and shot a minor official, Ernst vom Rath. This unleashed the pogrom known as ***Kristallnacht*** (the Night of Broken Glass) on 9 November 1938. Calling it a 'spontaneous outburst of rage', Hitler organised a full-scale attack on the Jews of Germany by Nazi Stormtroopers and activists. He gave orders to Gestapo and SS not to stop them.

The main targets were synagogues, shops and the homes of better off Jews. At least 1000 synagogues were burnt to the ground. The remaining Jewish-owned shops had their windows smashed – hence the name of the attack. Homes were broken into, Jews beaten up and their belongings destroyed. The success of five years of anti-Semitic propaganda can be judged from the fact that some bystanders joined in, while others expressed their approval. A girl in the Nazi 'League of German Girls', Melita Maschmann, was horrified by the damage but told herself:

> The Jews are the enemy of the new Germany. Last night they had a taste of what that means.

Unknown numbers of Jews were killed (perhaps 1000), several hundred committed suicide and 30,000 Jews were arrested that night and put in concentration camps, where many died. The German Jewish community had to pay a fine of 1 billion Reichsmarks. All Jewish taxpayers had to pay a 20 per cent levy. Insurance payments for the damage were confiscated. In December all Jewish businesses were compulsorily Aryanised. In February 1939 Jews had to hand over all personal jewellery and securities.

Turning point: *Kristallnacht*, 1938

Does *Kristallnacht* mark a turning point in the persecution of Jews? If so, in what ways?

As a means of forcing Jews out of Germany it was a success; one estimate is that 115,000 Jews left in the ten months between *Kristallnacht* and the outbreak of war in September 1939. The number of Jews left in Germany declined rapidly:

1937:	324,000
1938:	269,000
May 1939:	188,000
September 1939:	164,000.

Of those left, more than half were aged over 50. They were isolated, with no rights or any way of earning a living.

But there were still 164,000 of them. Hitler and his cronies, emboldened by how easy it had been, began to talk among themselves of taking even harsher measures.

Remember to record:

- changes in the way(s) Jews were persecuted, and the timing of these changes
- ways in which the Jews were treated differently from the other victims of the Nazis you have found out about already.

How did the war change Nazi anti-Semitism?

The short answers is, in two ways.

Firstly, the sheer numbers of Jews under Nazi rule grew enormously. Figures vary, but by the end of 1941 there were probably nearly 3.5 million Jews in Nazi-occupied Poland, 2.5 million in Nazi-occupied Russia and another 3 million in all the other countries taken over by the Nazis.

Secondly, the circumstances of war are very different from those of peacetime. With millions of armed invaders rampaging across the country civil society is suspended. What constitutes a crime, what is classed as permitted behaviour and attitudes towards life and death, are all affected. Hitler was well aware of this. The photograph shows what these ordinary soldiers – not necessarily Nazis – expected to do.

The German invasion of Poland began on 1 September 1939 and mass killings were carried out right from the start. As we have seen (pages 109–110), the victims included non-Jewish Poles as well, but Jews were singled out for special attention; no mercy was shown to the elderly, the sick, women and children. *Einsatzgrüppen* (Task Forces) or paramilitary units were formed to organise this killing and treated their victims with terrifying brutality, looting and setting fire to their homes before shooting them.

▷ German soldiers being transported by train to take part in the invasion of Poland. The graffiti reads: 'We're off to Poland to thrash the Jews.'

Young soldiers were the worst; they had experienced six years of anti-Semitic propaganda in their schools and the Hitler Youth. The violent personal humiliations of Jews employed by Nazis in Austria provided a precedent and an example: they were forced to clean the streets and toilets, men had their beards hacked off, women raped. Fifty thousand Jewish-Polish prisoners of war were kept in appalling conditions in a labour camp at Belzec. Half had died by early 1940. Many killings were also carried out by Polish anti-Semitic groups organised and controlled by SS commanders. Himmler told his men on 16 October 1939:

> You are the master race here ... Don't be soft, be merciless, and clear out everything that is not German and could hinder us in the work of re-construction.

He was referring here to Hitler's plan for conquered Poland. The last Polish units surrendered on 6 October and their country was split into three.

Area B was the General Government, controlled by Hans Frank, the leading Nazi lawyer. It became a German colony, where Poles had no rights at all. Frank set an example to his men by busily enriching himself, commandeering a castle to live in and a limousine to ride around in. Jews from Wartheland and all over the Reich – from Germany, Austria and Czechoslovakia – were sent to the General Government. From December 1939 they all had to wear the yellow star badge. Told they were being 're-settled', they found themselves herded into ghettos.

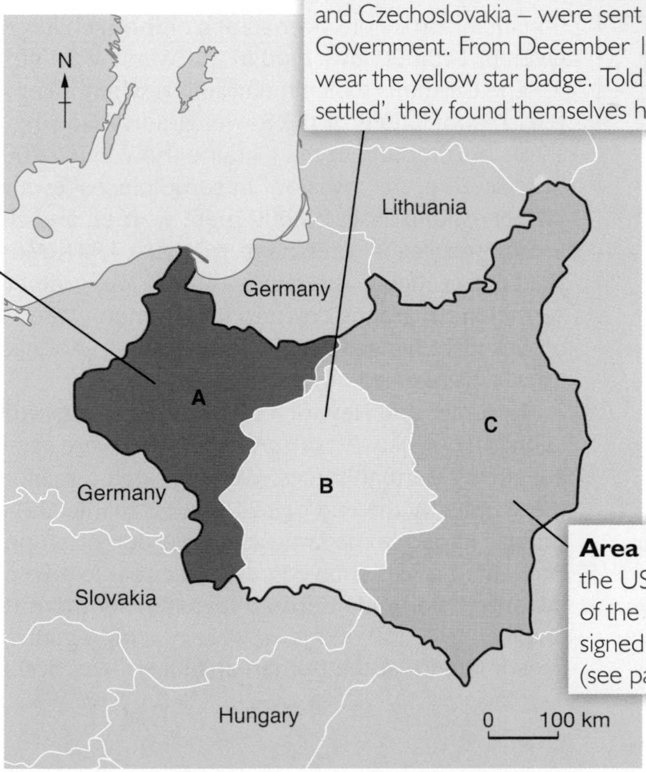

Area A was taken into the Reich, most of it named Wartheland. As part of Hitler's plan for *lebensraum*, living space, Poles and Jews were moved off farms and homes in this area to make way for German settlers.

Area C was taken over by the USSR under the terms of the Nazi-Soviet Pact signed in August 1939, (see page 82).

△ Poland 1939–41.

◁ **An elderly Jew being humiliated by a German military policeman (not, note, an SS member), in Warsaw, about 1940 or 1941.**

In many towns and cities in the General Government ghettos were created, confining the Jews into small areas, which were massively over-crowded. The largest was in Warsaw where, by early 1941, 446,000 people were crammed into a tiny section of the city of about 400 hectares, where they lived six or seven to a room. Diseases such as typhus and TB flourished in these conditions and the death rate soared among people weakened by lack of food. Emanuel Ringelblum, a historian who was a prisoner in the Warsaw Ghetto recorded in May 1941:

> One walks past the corpses with indifference. [They] are mere skeletons with a thin covering of skin over their bones.

Squabbles broke out over scraps of food, children begged on the streets. Overall, 140,000 Jews died in the Warsaw Ghetto.

The Germans took similar action when it came to dealing with the Jewish populations of the Soviet Union following the invasion of June 1941. In Lemburg, in the Ukraine (now Lviv), 7000 Jews were killed in the first weeks of the invasion. In some places Jews were clubbed to death. In Kamenetsk-Podolsk, 23,600 men, women and children were killed by the *Einsatzgrüppen* in three days in August 1941. Most notoriously, they drove Jews out of Kiev to the ravine of Babi Yar, ordered them to undress, then sent them in groups down to where men waited to shoot them . Soon the bodies were lying six or seven deep on top of each other in the ravine; 33,771 were killed.

Himmler and Heydrich drove their SS subordinates to step up the killings. Four new *Einsatzgrüppen* units were established behind the advancing German forces. Well over half a million Jews had been shot by these units by the end of 1941. In Lithuania and the Ukraine, anti-Semitic militias joined in the large-scale murder, often preceded by brutal beatings. Romanian forces showed particular zeal to take part in the killing as they advanced alongside German forces in southern Russia. In Odessa in October 1941, 19,000 Jews were machine-gunned by Romanian troops. It is estimated that the Romanians killed over 300,000 Jews.

■ **Turning point**: the war

Does the war mark a turning point in the persecution of Jews? If so, in what ways?

Ghettos were created in other areas too. In Vilnius, Lithuania, 29,000 Jews were forced into housing formerly accommodating 4000. Göbbels visited the ghetto in November 1941 and noted:

> The Jews are squatting amongst one another, horrible forms, not to be seen, let alone touched ... The Jews are the lice of civilised humanity. They have to be exterminated somehow.

Why did the Nazis change their policy towards the Jews in January 1942?

In January 1942 Heydrich called a conference of leading Nazi officials at Wannsee near Berlin. He reminded them that Göring had given him the task of arranging the 'Final Solution of the Jewish Question' in July 1941. He pointed out that there were 11 million Jews still alive in Europe, including Jews in countries outside German control, such as Ireland, Britain and Portugal. Plans had to be made to kill them all. This is the step from vicious persecution to **genocide**.

Although Hitler was not present at Wannsee he had been explicit about what he wanted to happen to Jewish people in speeches and conversations with other leading Nazis. In a speech in 1939 he had said: 'We are clear that the war can only end either by the Aryan peoples being exterminated or by Jewry disappearing from Europe.' Göbbels recorded a conversation he had with Hitler in December 1941:

> As far as the Jewish question is concerned, the Leader is determined to clear the decks. He prophesied to the Jews that if they brought about another world war, they would thereby experience their own annihilation.

Hitler's associates knew that the initiative now lay with them, by 'working towards the Führer' (see page 78) to carry this out.

Why did the policy towards the Jews change?

1 Hitler had been the driving force behind the increasing radicalisation of Nazi policy towards the Jews which we have seen over the last 8 pages. He was now master of most of Europe, from the English Channel almost to Moscow; there were no constraints on carrying his racial hatred to its conclusion.

2 The USA declared war on Germany on 11 December 1941. Hitler was convinced that the USA was run by Jews: 'Jewish-plutocrats', in parallel to the 'Jewish-Bolsheviks' who he believed controlled the Soviet Union.

3 The policy of mass shootings by *Einsatzgrüppen*, along with random killings, deaths in the ghettos and in labour and concentration camps, was too slow. It still left millions of Jews alive and there were signs of exhaustion among the killers.

There was therefore a need to increase the pace of killing and to find new methods of achieving its goal.

Words

Words are important.

The Final Solution
This policy was the deliberate killing of millions of human beings. For the Nazis, this uncomfortable fact was partly masked by calling it a 'solution' to a 'problem'.

Extermination
The word used for killing the Jews was the same German word as was used for killing vermin such as rats or bedbugs, usually translated as 'extermination'. As you will see, I prefer to use the words 'killing' and 'death'.

Genocide means the deliberate killing of a whole racial or ethnic group.

Did the Germans know?

After the war many Germans claimed not to have known what was happening to the Jews of Europe.

We now know that this is totally implausible. There were as many as 42,000 concentration camps by 1941, many in German cities with people living nearby. This magazine cover, from the *Nazi Illustrated Observer* featured pictures from inside the concentration camp at Dachau.

Then there were all those who played a part in carrying out the 'Final Solution', not just those who actually carried out the killings, but police, clerical staff and railway workers and those who lived near the camps and railway lines.

The Final Solution

The plan to put the 'Final Solution' into practice was called Operation Reinhard. It meant the building of death camps, eventually six of them, to kill Jews in large numbers. As you saw on page 108, the Nazis had already used carbon monoxide gas from vehicle exhausts to kill mentally and physically disabled people in their euthanasia programme, called Action T4. This programme had been halted in August 1941, so Action T4 personnel were available to use what they had learned.

All the death camps were in the former Poland, but with good rail links to Germany and the rest of Europe. The first was at Belzec and it was ready by February 1942. Within four weeks 75,000 Jews had been killed there, mainly from the ghettos of the General Government. The bodies were buried in huge pits. An Austrian SS officer, Franz Stangl, visited it in spring 1942:

> Oh God, the smell ... It was everywhere ... the pits ... full, they were full. I can't tell you; not hundreds, thousands of corpses. One of the pits had overflowed. They had put too many corpses in it and putrefaction had progressed too fast, so that the liquid underneath had pushed the bodies on top up and over and the corpses had rolled down the hill. Oh God it was awful.

Another death camp was built at Sobibor and was ready by May 1942. Within three months 100,000 had been killed there, from the General Government, Germany and Czechoslovakia. The death camps at Treblinka and Majdanek were in operation by July 1942. These four camps all used carbon monoxide gas from vehicle engines. After December 1942 the bodies were cremated, not buried. Between them, they are estimated to have killed 1,700,000 people by late 1943.

These death camps (and another at Chelmno) were quite small in area – Sobibor was only 12 hectares (30 acres). Auschwitz, on the other hand, was a huge complex. It included an IG Farben chemical works, accommodation for 7000 SS guards with a theatre and a pub, three large camps and 45 smaller ones. The death camp was at Birkenau, a few miles away from the main concentration and labour camps. Here gas chambers were built to kill 800 and 1200 people at once, using a gas called Zyklon-B. This was first used on 600 Soviet prisoners of war and then on Jews.

Jews from all over Europe were taken by train to Auschwitz over several days. They were transported in cattle trucks with inadequate food, water and sanitation. Many died on the journey. On arrival, guards hustled them out of the train and they were told to line up. On a ramp leading from the railway siding to the camp SS doctors selected those who were fit enough to work. The rest, including children, were taken by lorry straight to the gas chambers. These were disguised as showers and guards told them to undress to be 'disinfected'. Once inside the chamber the Zyklon-B was released. It took about 20 minutes before everyone was dead. Special detachments of Jewish prisoners then disentangled the bodies, removed any gold rings, or gold teeth, cut off the women's hair and sent the corpses by lift up to the cremating ovens.

Altogether, over 1,100,000 people were killed at Auschwitz, 90 per cent of them Jews. Jews were rounded up and sent there from all over German-occupied Europe: from France, Holland, Greece, Czechoslovakia, Belgium, Germany, Croatia, Italy, Belarus, Austria, Norway, Hungary and Greece.

In total, around six million Jews were killed by the Nazis. This was about two-thirds of the Jewish population of Europe in 1939.

Turning point: the Wannsee Conference, 1942

Does the Wannsee Conference (page 119) mark a turning point in the persecution of Jews? If so, in what ways?

Having analysed the four turning points given, can you identify any other moments in the history of the Nazi treatment of Jews which should also be regarded as a turning point?

Complete the final row of your copy of the table shown on page 101, recording the treatment of Jews.

Concluding your Enquiry

Look over your completed table. Use the evidence you have gathered to make some comparisons.

1. What similarities or differences can you see in the nature and the timing of the persecution of the groups and in the way their persecution changed over time?
2. Now focus particularly on the Jews and consider questions such as these:
   - Were they persecuted for different reasons?
   - Were they persecuted on a different timescale?
   - Around 6 million Jews were killed by the Nazis. Why were so many killed?
   - Is the only difference between the Jews and other persecuted groups a matter of numbers?
3. Now write your answer to the big enquiry question: In what ways were Jews treated differently from other victims of Nazism?

Germania: the capital of the world

In January 1938 newspapers in Germany and across the world marvelled at a dramatic new set of plans that had been unveiled for the rebuilding of the German capital, Berlin. The architect of those plans was Albert Speer, who by then was well on his way to becoming one of Hitler's closest and most trusted advisers.

Speer's plans for Berlin were breathtaking. He had designed what Hitler had imagined. The Führer had never been proud of Berlin and despised the sort of people who lived there. This was the city that fostered liberal ideas during the Weimar Republic and the 'Golden Twenties'. It was a city that celebrated modern art, new styles of music, and held wild parties at fashionable clubs. Compared with other European cities of the 1920s, Berlin permitted a more relaxed attitude towards homosexuals and had several gay bars. In the elections of 1932 and 1933, only a quarter of Berliners voted for the Nazi Party. Hitler was more than happy that the old Berlin should be swept away. He even joked that British air raids in 1940 were simply helping prepare the ground for his great new capital, a capital that would be given a new name, Germania.

If the Reich that Hitler was creating was to last a thousand years and rival that of the British Empire and the ancient Roman Empire, then the capital city needed to reflect this. He declared that Germania would 'be comparable only with ancient Egypt, Babylon or Rome. What is London, what is Paris by comparison?' For inspiration, Hitler looked to the architecture of ancient Greece and Rome. Sure enough, Speer's plans displayed the form of architecture known as neo-classicism, following the structures of the classical world.

Speer produced a magnificent model to show off his plans for the new city. Its crowning glory was to be the *Volkshalle* or Peoples' Hall. The image opposite shows this from a carefully lit part of Speer's model. The hall was to be the largest enclosed space in the world, designed to seat 180,000 people underneath its massive dome. Concerns were expressed that the breath of an audience in the building might create its own weather system! Outside the dome there was to be an Avenue of Splendours that would run north–south through the Brandenburg Gate to become a parade ground, free of traffic. There would also be an Arch of Triumph large enough to fit the Parisian Arc de Triomphe under its span. On the instructions of Hitler, the name of every one of the 1.8 million German soldiers who had died in the 1914–18 war was to be inscribed on its walls.

Speer had no worries about planning permission as no one could oppose Hitler's clear wishes. Nor did he need concern himself too much over materials or labour. Brick and stone would come from large quarries worked by a company owned by the SS. Labour would be provided from the concentration camps. With the war under way, Speer had a total workforce of 130,000 labouring on his project, including 30,000 Russian prisoners of war captured in Germany's early successes in its invasion of the Soviet Union.

But for all the planning and the preparation of the ground, only one of Speer's buildings was ever completed: the new Reichstag Chancellery – and even this was destroyed by British bombs in the final months of the war. Hitler's Thousand Year Reich that was founded in 1933 had lasted no more than twelve years. By May 1945 its capital city was a mockery of the intended glories of Germania. Berlin lay in ruins and Hitler was dead.

From 1946 to 1966, Speer was imprisoned in Spandau Prison to the west of Berlin following the Nuremberg Trials of senior Nazis after the war. During that time, he wrote his memoirs *Inside the Third Reich*. It was there that he used the phrase *Welthauptstadt* (the capital of the world) to describe Germania. Even Hitler had not claimed this for his new city!

9 Why didn't Germany surrender earlier?

General Friedrich Paulus, commander of the German Sixth Army at Stalingrad, radio message to Adolf Hitler, 24 January 1943:

Troops without ammunition or food. Effective command no longer possible. 18,000 wounded without any supplies or dressings or drugs. Further defence senseless. Collapse inevitable. Army requests immediate permission to surrender in order to save lives of remaining troops.

Adolf Hitler, radio message to Friedrich Paulus, 24 January 1943:

Surrender is forbidden. Sixth Army will hold their positions to the last man and the last round and by their heroic endurance will make an unforgettable contribution toward the establishment of a defensive front and the salvation of the Western world.

In August 1942 the German army advanced on the city of Stalingrad, 2000 km into south-east USSR. The aim was to seize Stalingrad and move on to the vitally important Caucasus oilfields. They nearly succeeded. However, the Red Army fought a bitter hand-to-hand resistance in the streets and buildings of the city and then their fresh armies encircled the German forces. Cut off from all supplies, his depleted army suffering from intense cold, disease and hunger, their commander, Friedrich Paulus, surrendered on 31 January 1943. Two hundred and fifty thousand German soldiers had been killed, 91,000 became prisoners of war.

Hearing the dire news from Stalingrad, several German commanders confided to each other that they could see that they would now lose the war. During the initial invasion of Russia, Soviet casualties had been three times heavier than German losses; at Stalingrad they were about equal. The Red Army was much bigger, could draw on a larger population, had more aeroplanes, more tanks and industrial plant safe in the east producing war material faster and in greater quantities than Germany. Red Army generals, after their disastrous performance in 1941, had obviously learned how to use their superiority.

Elsewhere, German forces had been defeated by British forces at El Alamein in North Africa in November 1942 and the Allies were planning the landings in Sicily which took place in July 1943. US industry was fully organised for war, outstripping even the Soviets. Britain was now producing more planes than Germany and their heavy bombing of German cities had been going on since March 1942.

Yet the Nazis kept on fighting for over two more years after the defeat at Stalingrad before surrendering on 8 May 1945.

The cost of this determination to fight to the end was a catastrophe for the German people. Three million soldiers and half a million civilians were killed. Millions more Jews were murdered. Hitler, Himmler, Göbbels (with his wife and all their six children) and many other leading Nazis committed suicide, but so did thousands of civilians, sometimes entire families taking poison or drowning themselves together.

Many beautiful German towns and cities were reduced to rubble, with what was left of their populations clinging on in the ruins. Devastation and pain was felt all over Germany, but, at various points in this final enquiry we will focus especially on Berlin, the once busy, sophisticated, fun-loving capital. What did it mean for Berlin and its people to fight on for two more years?

◁ Russian Red Army soldiers clamber over the rubble outside the ruins of the Reichstag in Berlin on 2 May 1945. Compare this image with Hitler's plans for Berlin on pages 122–123.

Enquiry Focus: Why didn't Germany surrender earlier?

Professor Richard Evans calls such refusal to surrender 'without precedent'. In virtually all wars throughout history the losing side recognises that they have lost, and surrenders in order to save what is left of their country and their people.

In this last enquiry you will find it helpful to draw on aspects of Nazism you have discovered in this book. They will help you answer the big enquiry question: Why didn't Germany surrender earlier?

As you read through the sombre story of the last two years of the Third Reich, you will be able to infer a number of reasons why the war went on so long. Some will be down to 'Faith', such as belief in Hitler, in Nazism, in the German Fatherland. Some will be down to 'Fear': fear of what would happen if they surrendered, fear of what the Nazis would do to them if they didn't go on fighting and fear of the consequences of defeat informed by bad memories of the defeat in 1918. And some reasons you may want to define for yourself. We will break the story of the last years of the war into five sections. In each section you will be searching for evidence to put under the headings of Faith, Fear or Other Factors. The five sections are:

1. The German Army
2. Hitler
3. The Nazi Party
4. The German people
5. The Russians

1. The German Army and the continuation of the war

After Stalingrad the German Army fought on for another 27 months. The westward advance of the Red Army, the Allied forces pushing north through Italy and then, after D-Day in June 1944 eastwards through France, were all made to fight for every mile. There were counter-attacks and lines held, defences organised. Why was the army prepared to fight on so stubbornly?

See page 24 for the way imperial **values** survived among the officer class under Weimar.

The high command consisted of older men, born in the 1880s and 1890s, who had been brought up in the Kaiser's Imperial Army, its long training imbuing **values** of obedience, loyalty, patriotism and honour. These values survived virtually unchanged into the army under Weimar. Major-General Bruhn commented to his fellow officers in November 1944: 'The Officer Corps loves its country, and believes implicitly in its own respectability and ideas of honour, and lives accordingly.' Field Marshall Model told his men in July 1944: 'Cowards have no place in our ranks, it's about our homeland, our wives and children.' It was the same in the navy. Admiral Dönitz insisted, as late as March 1945: 'Our honour demands that we fight to the last.' This belief that death was preferable to surrender was deeply-rooted.

The bomb plot in July 1944 (see below) was a huge embarrassment to the officer class. The plotters were army officers and had broken one of the basic rules of the unwritten code: unquestioning obedience to the German government – whoever that might be. Many senior officers were not Nazis and were uneasy about what the Nazis were doing. After the plot they were anxious to make amends for the army by asserting their loyalty to Hitler. General Jödl described the day of the failed plot as 'the blackest day in German history' and called on his fellow generals to 'gather round the Führer at the last, so that we may be justified before posterity'.

In December 1943 Hitler had set up a system of National Socialist Leadership Officers (*Nationalsozialistischer Führungsoffizier* – NSFOs). They were to ensure that all soldiers, including officers, were fully aware of Nazi ideals and acted in accordance with them. Indeed, loyalty became a more important quality than military ability.

Junior officers were of course younger, mostly born after 1910. They shared their superiors' code of values, and were, like them, largely Protestants (unlike the ordinary soldiers, the majority of whom were Roman Catholics). However, junior officers had received much more Nazi indoctrination, at school and in the Hitler Youth; 43 per cent of them were Nazi Party members.

What about the rank and file of the army? It is hard to generalise about an army numbering several millions. Allied psychologists interviewed captured German soldiers towards the end of the war and calculated that about 35 per cent were Nazi supporters, within which 10 per cent were described as 'fanatics'.

This division is reflected in the research historians have carried out using the letters written by soldiers to their families. Many simply expressed a wish to get home safely. Convinced Nazis wrote things like:

> We, the entire German people, stand fast in a fierce struggle against these degenerate people, led by Jewish parasites.

Less ideological, more patriotic, were views such as:

> I believe for certain that a change will come. On no account will we capitulate! That so much blood has already been spilt in this freedom fight cannot be in vain. The war can and will end in German victory!

Censors struck out any talk of defeat, or lack of support for Hitler, but some of these views got through:

> Providence has determined the destruction of the German people and Hitler is the executor of this will.

As late as January 1945, 62 per cent of captured German soldiers expressed their faith in Hitler; however, by March this had fallen dramatically, to 21 per cent.

Clearly, even though they were retreating almost continuously, even though 1.8 million German soldiers were killed in 1944, the army held together remarkably well – for whatever reasons. It was only in 1945, as enemy forces advanced into and through their country, that many soldiers lost the will to fight. Casualty rates were horribly high in these months: one-third of all German losses in the entire war took place in the last four and a half months. Many soldiers put down their weapons and went home: an estimated half a million soldiers deserted in 1945. To make your escape was risky as courts martial carried out rapid executions of deserters. Often the bodies of hanged deserters were left hanging as a warning to others, with a notice round their neck such as 'I am a coward' or 'I am a deserter and have failed to protect German women and children'. From February 1945, 'flying courts martial', consisting of a judge, an army officer and a Nazi Party member carried out rapid executions. After the war one of the judges explained this application of Nazi legal principles:

> Whatever serves the people is just ... it follows that whatever serves the army is just ... The commonest offence bringing men before the firing squad was desertion, which led to 15,000 executions ... Sentences were carried out as soon as possible after being passed ... The faster a pest in the armed forces receives the punishment he has deserved ... the easier it will be to maintain manly discipline among the troops.

Look back to what you found out about Nazi justice in Chapter 5.

It is worth looking at some comparisons for those figures: 18 German soldiers were shot for desertion in the First World War; in the Second World War the British Army executed 40, the French 103 and the US 146 soldiers for desertion.

With so many Germans lying dead on the battlefields of Europe, Hitler drew on the last resources of manpower left, calling up all males aged 16 to 60 into the *Volksstürm* (People's Storm), launched in October 1944, (among them, Alfons Heck – see pages 2–3). Idealistically, these boys and older men, having sworn a personal oath of loyalty to Hitler, fighting on their home territory, would heroically hold up the enemy, buying some time. In time, perhaps the Allies would fall out among themselves, or the

■ Now make your notes on why the German Army did not surrender earlier. Use the three headings Faith, Fear and Other Factors.

'miracle weapons' would arrive. In fact, the People's Storm was seen by many as evidence of how desperate the Nazis were. Could the defence of the Reich now depend on teenagers on bicycles with anti-tank weapons, or wielding machine guns bigger than they were? In Berlin in March 1945 the age limit was lowered to 14 and girls were recruited. With no uniforms and a shortage of weapons, the People's Storm were militarily useless. Everyone tried to avoid serving and desertion was rife. Nevertheless, 175,000 'soldiers' of the People's Storm were killed in the seven months of its existence.

2. Hitler and the continuation of the war

What happened to Mussolini?

Benito Mussolini had been dictator of Italy since 1922. In the early days of the Nazi Party Hitler had admired him and they formed the Rome-Berlin Axis in 1936.

By 1943 the war was going very badly for Italy. In July, Allied forces landed in Sicily and Rome was bombed for the first time. In addition, Italians were suffering from food shortages, industry was at a standstill for lack of raw materials and workers were on strike.

Mussolini was forced to call the Fascist Grand Council, which had not met since 1939 and normally supported him. The Council voted to ask the King, who was still the head of the Italian state, to take over. Mussolini was arrested the next day. Italy made peace with the Allies in September 1943.

Mussolini was eventually killed by communist partisans while trying to escape from Italy in April 1945.

Hitler's ally and fellow-dictator, Benito Mussolini, had been forced out of office. Why didn't the same happen to Hitler?

Although there were some similarities between conditions in Italy and Germany in 1943, there were some even more important differences.

The King of Italy was head of the Italian state and so had authority over Mussolini. When it came to the crunch, Mussolini was forced out. In Germany Hitler had combined the roles of Chancellor and President (head of the German state) when Hindenburg died in 1934. Since then, no one had authority over him: he was the Führer.

In Germany, there was no such body as the Fascist Grand Council where opposition to the ruling party could gather. The Council of Ministers had not met since 1938; the Reichstag had long ceased to be a democratic body and met for the last time in 1942 to hand over all power to Hitler. All the leading Nazis were utterly dependent on Hitler and he had deliberately created rivalries between them, so they would not combine together to oppose him. He had no second-in-command.

Look again at Chapter 6, especially pages 74–77, to remind yourself about this personal dicatorship, the *führerprinzip*.

Hitler was therefore in complete control and his views became German policy. One of his most deeply held instincts was to avoid what he believed had happened to his country in 1918.

Memories of the 'stab in the back'

As you know, in September 1918 the Imperial Army's Supreme Command told the Kaiser that Germany was facing certain defeat. In a cynical move, the generals suggested handing over power to the democratic politicians, who would then have to take the blame for making peace.

This is exactly what happened. The power and prestige of the Imperial Army, the lack of free information under the Kaiser's government, meant that none of the ordinary soldiers or civilians was aware of the military situation. When it came, the Armistice of November 1918 was a shock to most Germans; to Hitler it was a traumatic event which became one of the rocks on which he built all his guiding principles. He fully believed and propagated the myths of 1918: that the army had been '**stabbed in the back**' by the politicians, labelled the November Criminals for arranging the 'disgraceful' peace. Facing military defeat himself in 1945, **Hitler** was determined that the 'disgrace' of surrender would not happen again.

See pages 11 and 19 for more on the '**stab in the back**'.

Look again at page 18 to remind yourself how bitter **Hitler** felt in 1918.

The bomb plot, July 1944

The only other possible source of power in Germany apart from Hitler was the Army. His relationship with senior generals was close. He had made himself supreme commander of the armed forces in 1938 and in December 1941 sacked his senior generals and took over personal command of the war on the Eastern Front. He had moved to his heavily-fortified headquarters, the Wolf's Lair (*Wolfsschanze*) at Rastenburg in East Prussia, 600 km east of Berlin, (now in Poland) in June 1941 and spent over 800 days there in the next three and a half years.

His relationship with his generals was uneasy. He favoured bold, daring actions and supported generals with the same approach. He abused more cautious commanders, calling them cowardly, narrow-minded and stupid. In August 1942, General Halder recorded in his diary:

> Discussions with the Führer today were once more characterised by serious accusations levelled against the military leadership. They are accused of intellectual arrogance, incorrigibility and an inability to recognise the essentials.

Halder was dismissed the next month. While the war was going well, everyone admired Hitler and began to call him a 'military genius'. When things started to go badly wrong his lack of military experience began to show. He was stubborn, often indecisive, obsessed with detail. He disliked listening to information which did not correspond with what he thought ought to be the situation. Thousands of men were lost through his inability to order strategic retreats. Eventually he lived in his own world of maps, detached from reality, giving orders to battalions which no longer existed.

And so, late in his dictatorship, army officers began to murmur about removing him. Some were motivated by shame and disgust at the mass murders being carried out in their country's name, while others, including those who had themselves led *Einsatzgrüppen* units (see pages 116–118), were simply concerned about the prospect of total defeat. Given Hitler's position, the only way things could be changed was by assassinating him.

1. How did the failure of the bomb plot affect the conduct of the war after July 1944?
2. Now make your notes on how the personality and role of Hitler kept Germany from surrendering. Use the three headings Faith, Fear and Other Factors.

The only plotter able to get near enough to Hitler to carry this out was Claus von Stauffenburg. As one of the Chiefs of Staff, he had access to the Wolf's Lair and on 20 July 1944 planted a briefcase-bomb in Hitler's map-room. However, the briefcase was moved away from Hitler and he survived with only minor injuries. The plot collapsed and savage reprisals began. Altogether about 5000 people were arrested; these included those who knew about the plot but had said nothing but also, according to the Nazi law of 'blood guilt', the close relatives of the plotters. Between 500 and 1000 people were shot, hanged or committed suicide. Göbbels had the hangings filmed.

The aftermath of the plot sealed Germany's fate. The Army sought to demonstrate their loyalty to Hitler in order, as Colonel-General Reinhardt put it, to 'justify his trust'. Perhaps surprisingly, there was an outpouring of expressions of relief for Hitler's survival. 'Thank God the Führer is alive!' and 'What would we have done without the Führer?' people were reported as saying. The country was now locked into Hitler's fate for them.

3. The Nazi Party and the continuation of the war

The Neues Museum (New Museum, which was new in 1859) in Berlin holds thousands of unique archaeological exhibits collected by German archaeologists. It was heavily damaged in 1945 and did not re-open until 2009. When I visited it in 2012 there was still a line of machine-gun bullet holes at about chest height all along the columns at the front of the building and in the wall behind them. They were evidence that Nazi fanatics had been mown down as they staged a last stand in the very heart of Berlin. They had decided that, like most Nazis, they had nothing to gain by surrender.

In 1943, the UK Prime Minister Churchill and US President Roosevelt met at Casablanca and agreed that their terms for the end of the war were the unconditional surrender of the Nazi regime. By 1944 the Nazi Party was the government of Germany. At the top, with Hitler away at the Front and reluctant to make decisions anyway, four leading Nazis ran the country, passing regulations which had the effect of laws. These were Himmler, Göbbels, Bormann and Speer. (Göring's star had waned as the *Luftwaffe* had failed to control the skies as he had promised.) Regional governments had been taken over by local Nazi Party bosses, the *gauleiter*. Given the Allies' demand for unconditional surrender, all these men knew that there was no future for them if the Allies won the war. They also knew that they were deeply tainted by the plunder, terror and murder which had been carried out both by the Party as the government and themselves as individuals.

Plunder

Many Nazi officials had used their positions for personal gain. Hans Frank, for example, the Nazi Governor of Poland, lived in luxury in the former Polish royal palace at Cracow. He helped himself to goods looted in Poland

and embezzled from government funds. He had two warehouses full of furs, chocolate, coffee and spirits; in November 1940 alone he sent to his several homes in Germany a consignment consisting of 72 kilos of beef, 20 geese, 50 hens and 50 kilos of cheese. All over Germany, Nazi bosses had used the unlimited power they held as an opportunity to get rich. They took over Jewish businesses at rock bottom prices during the **Aryanisation** process, or took bribes to ensure their friends did. They looted, or took over, the homes of Jews forced into exile. Their lifestyle gained them the nickname 'golden pheasants' from the suffering German people.

Look again at page 114 to remind yourself how **Aryanisation** took place.

Leading Nazis preferred more cultural plunder. Hitler intended to set up an art gallery in his home town of Linz to rival the great galleries of Europe. He employed an art expert to see that his collection consisted of the best that could be seized from the capital cities and Jewish-held private collections of occupied Europe. Göring travelled personally to Paris to select 27 masterpieces from the Louvre and Jeu de Paume galleries, including several paintings by Rembrandt, Leonardo da Vinci and Breughel. He had amassed a personal fortune of 200 million Reichsmarks and used some of it to build a huge 'Hunting Lodge', the Carinhall.

Terror

We saw in Chapters 5 and 8 that real Nazi terror was visited almost exclusively on their racial victims and conquered people, not Germans themselves. In the last months of the war, as defeat drew near and the Nazis realised that they had nothing to gain by surrender, everyone in Germany became subject to Nazi terror.

Look at page 57 to remind yourself about the role of the Gestapo in the peacetime years.

Party members were issued with weapons. Bormann instructed them that anyone leaving their post would be subject to 'the most severe punishment' and that 'Signs of disintegration would be ruthlessy nipped in the bud'. In the final months, the flying courts martial described on page 127 began to be used throughout Germany by Nazi fanatics determined that their enemies were not to enjoy their defeat. Criticism of Hitler could bring instant arrest and execution on the spot. In Heilbronn, for example, in April 1945, a man who had distributed anti-Nazi pamphlets in 1933 and another man who had shouted 'Drop dead Hitler', probably while drunk, were arrested, taken from their cells by local Nazis to a wood outside town, and shot. Talk of surrender or showing a white flag, even as Allied forces drew near, could get you shot. A shadowy organisation calling itself Werwolf carried out killings of anti-Nazis, continuing to do so even after the surrender.

The historian Ian Kershaw describes what happened at the town of Ansbach on 18 April 1945. With US troops only hours away, a young theology student sought to avoid the destruction and loss of life that continued – and pointless – fighting would bring. He cut the telephone wires connecting the local Nazi commandant with the army unit outside the town. He was spotted by two Hitler Youth boys, who informed the police. The student was arrested, given a two-minute 'trial' and sentenced to death. He was hanged in full view of the local people. Four hours later US troops entered Ansbach.

The Death Marches

Yet at the same time, and even as defeat loomed, the Nazis tried to hide the worst of their systems for mass murder. Belzec, Treblinka and Sobibor death camps were closed in 1943, their sites grassed over, the buildings demolished, in an attempt to hide what had happened there. Killings, however, continued at Chelmno until summer 1944 and at Auschwitz until November, after which the gas chambers were hurriedly demolished. The Red Army arrived at Auschwitz on 27 January 1945, to find just 7000 emaciated prisoners in a slave-labour camp that once held 140,000. On 17 January nearly 60,000 prisoners had been evacuated westwards to another camp: 56,000 on foot, 2200 by train in open coal wagons. The prisoners were already in a weakened state; there was little food or water; it was the dead of winter; the guards were jumpy, ill-disciplined and scared of falling into the hands of the Russians. Anyone falling behind was shot. Conditions at the camp they eventually reached were terrible:

> We are a thousand men lying in a room with space for a maximum of two hundred. We can't wash, we get half a litre of swede-broth and 200 grams of bread. Up to today there are 250 dead in our barracks alone.

They were then sent westwards on journeys of many days by train. At least 15,000 died out of those who set off from Auschwitz.

This was just one of dozens of forced marches which became known as Death Marches following Himmler's instructions in January 1945 to evacuate all concentration camps, prisons and prisoner of war camps in the path of the Red Army. He gave the order, but could not provide the means to carry it out. There were still 700,000 people in concentration camps at that time, most of whom were either Jews or Russian prisoners. The situation in Poland and eastern Germany was chaotic, with the roads full of fleeing refugees, prisoners and abandoned vehicles, and many dead bodies lying at the side.

▷ Slave labour by concentration camp prisoners clearing up in Bremen after a bombing raid.

By April 1945 the camps in the shrinking area of Germany still under Nazi control had become grossly over-crowded. The number of prisoners at Buchenwald, for example, rose from 37,000 in 1943 to 100,000 by January 1945. Numbers at Bergen-Belsen gradually increased from about 4000 in 1944. Anne Frank arrived there in October from Auschwitz and died of typhus in March 1945. By then there were 60,000 people in the camp. The food ran out completely and the SS guards made little effort to deal with the situation. From the beginning of 1945 to 15 April, when the British Army took over the camp and restored water and food supplies, 35,000 had died. Another 14,000 were too weak or ill to recover.

In the chaos surrounding the fall of Nazi Germany accurate figures are hard to establish, but as many as 350,000 may well have died on the Death Marches and in the remaining concentration camps – half of whom were alive at the beginning of 1945.

The end of the Nazis

Hitler was only 56 when he committed suicide. He had become detached from the events surrounding him, convinced that he had been let down by the generals, and eventually by the German people. He never visited the Front, nor any of the bombed out cities. He seemed a much older man: he was taking up to 28 pills a day for various ailments, his hands shook with Parkinson's Disease, he walked with a stoop, was so short-sighted that documents had to be typed with specially large print and he sometimes dribbled when he spoke. But Germany faced no alternative but to follow the path he had set.

On 29 April, as Red Army troops got to the Potsdammer Platz, less than 500 yards from his bunker, Hitler prepared to end his life. He gave poison to his dog, Blondi, married Eva Braun, and then, on the afternoon of 30 April, shot himself. Braun took poison. His personal assistants burned their bodies, watched by Bormann and Göbbels.

That same evening, Göbbels and his wife Magda, gave their six children injections to put them to sleep, then crushed cyanide pills in their mouths. Magda had written:

> The world that will come after the Leader and National Socialism will not be worth living in, and therefore I have taken my children away. They are too dear to endure what is coming next … We have now only one aim: loyalty unto death to the Leader.

Many more leading Nazis killed themselves. The last two generals with Hitler shot themselves, along with the commander of his escort. Bormann took poison to avoid capture by the Russians. Himmler committed suicide when he was captured by the British. Ley hanged himself before his trial at Nuremberg. Göring went through his trial, then committed suicide the night before he was due to be hanged. The last Nazi suicide was Rudolf Hess. Sentenced to life imprisonment, he hanged himself in 1987, aged 93.

1 How did the Allies' demand for unconditional surrender affect the decision of the Nazi leaders not to surrender?

2 What do the attempts to hide the death camps and the suicide of many leading Nazis tell you about their attitude to defeat?

3 Why did the Nazi leaders decide that they had nothing to gain by surrendering?

■ Now make your notes on how the Nazi Party kept Germany from surrendering. Use the three headings Faith, Fear and Other Factors.

4. The German people and the continuation of the war

On the night of 24/25 July 1943 over 700 British aircraft bombed the city of Hamburg. It was bombed again the next day by US planes, and then three times more by British bombers over the next ten nights. Altogether, 9000 tons of bombs were dropped on the city. The weight of bombs, many of which were incendiaries, set fire to 8 square miles of buildings. The heat was intense, reaching 800 degrees, and produced a new phenomenon: a firestorm. The blaze sucked in air, creating hurricane-force hot winds which tore down trees. The firestorm also sucked air out of the air-raid shelters, where hundreds died of carbon monoxide poisoning.

The concerted Allied bombing campaign began in January 1943, with the intention of destroying German industrial production and breaking the morale of the German people. The industrial cities of the Ruhr were the first targets, with the Dam Busters raid in May 1943. Other towns and cities followed, not all of them industrial targets.

Some preparations had been made: air-raid wardens were appointed, blackout regulations enforced, searchlights and anti-aircraft guns set up. Shelters were built, but disbelief that they would be needed meant that there were too few. Supplies of concrete were hard to come by, so it was often only the private shelters of Nazi bosses which got built. In the early part of the war anti-aircraft defences and German night-fighters inflicted heavy losses on the RAF and even heavier losses on US daylight raiders. However, as the war went on the strength of the *Luftwaffe* waned and by 1945 Allied planes met little opposition. Of the 1.42 million tons of bombs dropped on Germany in the war, 1.12 million tons fell in the last 12 months of the war. Thousands died: 35,000 in Dresden in January 1945. Out of a population of only 79,000, 17,000 died in a 22-minute raid on Pforzheim in February. In total, probably 450,000 were killed by Allied bombing.

▽ Berlin's buildings reduced to shells after the bombing caused firestorms.

Berlin was heavily bombed in November 1943. Seven hundred bombers brought Berlin's own firestorm. Nine thousand citizens were killed, and 812,000 made homeless. As elsewhere, shelters were too few and too small. Admission was by identity card, which Berlin's foreign workers and remaining Jews did not possess. Warnings of air-raids grew shorter as German radar failed, and panic set in. In January 1944, 35 people died in the rush to get into the shelter in the Hermannplatz. Hitler's Berlin bunker was 40 feet beneath the Reich Chancellery, on two floors, with its own generator, water and heating and a 12-foot thick concrete roof. Together with his other two bunkers, it had used more concrete than all the shelter construction for the rest of Germany for 1943 and 1944 combined.

Typically, Berliners in the shelters turned their anxiety and resentment of the Nazis into jokes:

> 'Who do we have to thank for the night fighters?'
>
> 'Hermann Göring!'
>
> 'For the whole air force?'
>
> 'Hermann Göring!'
>
> 'On whose orders did Hermann Göring do all this?'
>
> 'The Führer!'
>
> 'Where would we be if it were not for Hermann Göring and the Führer?'
>
> 'In our beds!'

From then on, life in Berlin became a matter of survival in the ruins. Only the cellars of many buildings were inhabitable. The electricity supply became steadily more erratic, and was hardly available at all by the end of the war. Water too was only occasionally turned on at street pumps. Berliners, usually women, queued for hours, hoping to get to the tap with their pail before the water supply ran out.

Gender roles changed in these situations. Women, put in the position of fragile home-makers by Nazi propaganda, found that they had the determination to survive. One Berlin diarist noted a growing toughness:

> Over and over again during these days I've been noticing that not only my feelings, but those of all women towards men have changed. We are sorry for them, they seem so pathetic and lacking in strength. The weaker sex. A kind of collective disappointment among women seems to be growing under the surface. The male-dominant Nazi world, glorifying the strong man, is tottering ...

Children's lives changed completely. Some Berlin children were evacuated, but not on the organised scale of evacuation in Britain. Many families arranged their own evacuation, sending their children to relatives in the countryside. Schools began to close in the afternoons, so that pupils could help with tasks such as filling sandbags or helping their families. Many schools were bombed and by 1944 hardly any schooling took place at all. By then, as we saw on pages 127–128 children as young as sixteen could be called up into the People's Storm – by 1945, even fourteen-year-olds. Historian Antony Beevor tells of fourteen-year-old Erich Schmidtke who was called up as a 'flak-helper' to man anti-aircraft guns. Ordered to report to the Hermann Göring barracks, his mother helped him pack his little suitcase and went with him. After three days in the barracks they were ordered to assemble at the Reichssportsfeld in the west of Berlin. He decided to desert and went into hiding until the war was over. Most of those who had joined with him were killed.

Total War

In February 1943, soon after the terrible defeat at Stalingrad, Göbbels declared that Germany was now to wage a Total War. He had been calling for this policy for some time, but until then Hitler had resisted him. One of Hitler's beliefs about the ignominious defeat of 1918 was that hardship at home had led to the revolutions which 'stabbed the Army in the back', so he tried to protect civilian living standards. In July Göbbels was made **Reich Plenipotentiary** for Total War. Working hours were increased and women up to the age of 55 could be drafted to work in factories. Businesses defined as 'non-essential' were closed down and workers re-deployed to factories or the armed forces. This meant that many of Berlin's famous bars and cafés had to close as waiters were re-deployed. One million more men had been sent to the Front by December.

Plenipotentiary: having full and complete power.

By 1945 there were severe food shortages as well. Rationing had been introduced even before the war and as preparation for it, in 1937. It covered clothing and shoes as well as food. There were different levels of ration, depending on your position – and your race. Those doing heavy labouring work received the best rations, with the armed forces allocated more than ordinary civilians. Foreign workers from western Europe came next, with those from the east receiving barely enough to live on. Rations for Jews were the least of all, and were eventually withdrawn entirely. However, after 1943 rations for every group were reduced. The ration for civilians for meat, for example, was 2400 grams a month in 1939, 1600 grams by 1941 and 550 grams by January 1945. And that was if you could get it! Most people spent long hours in queues and the black market flourished. Exchanging goods and services by barter became common. Mathilde Wolff-Mönckeberg recorded, in March 1944:

> I have exchanged the table for fat and meat … You can only persuade workmen into your house if you press cigarettes into their hands or treat them to a glass of brandy.

The amount of petty thefts, of food and warm clothes, increased, assisted by the **blackout** and the increasing chaos into which urban life had fallen.

In order not to assist Allied bombers seeking their targets, no streetlights were lit and all houses had to have thick curtains – this was known as the '**blackout**'.

The great Russian writer and journalist Vassily Grossman recorded the scene of chaos and destruction he saw as he entered Berlin with the Red Army just before the end of the war:

> I had a terrible mass of impressions. Fires and smoke, smoke, smoke. Huge crowds of prisoners of war. Faces are full of tragedy and the grief on many faces is not only personal suffering but also that of a citizen of a destroyed country …
>
> This overcast, cold and rainy day is undoubtedly the day of Germany's collapse in smoke, among the blazing ruins, among hundreds of corpses littering the streets. [He saw an old dead woman whose] head leant against the wall, sitting on a mattress near a front door, with an expression of quiet and everlasting grief. [Nearby, the Russians were amazed at the thoroughness of German housewives] In the streets which are already quiet, the ruins are being tidied and swept. Women are sweeping pavements with brooms …

By then millions of Germans were living in cellars and ruins, with no water and no power, their lives a daily struggle for food. Reports described people's attitudes as 'fatalistic' and 'helpless'. However much they now hated the Nazis, life was far too difficult for there to be a popular rising against them.

■ Now make your notes on how the German people themselves helped keep Germany from surrendering. Use the three headings Faith, Fear and Other Factors.

5. The Russians and the continuation of the war

As the Red Army advanced inexorably westwards, and then, in October 1944, set foot on the sacred soil of the Fatherland, many Germans became deeply afraid. They knew what their army had done during the invasion of the USSR. Soldiers on leave told their friends and families what they had seen, or even taken part in. Most people knew about the burnt villages, the looting of homes, the slaughtered peasants, the Russian prisoners of war left to starve to death, the mass shootings of Jews. Then, as the German army retreated out of the USSR, they had destroyed everything behind them: homes, crops, bridges, railway tracks.

Soviet propaganda made full use of these horrors to urge on the Red Army: 'Take merciless revenge on the fascist child murderers and executioners, pay them back for the blood and tears of soviet mothers and children!' they raged. Their soldiers were only too ready to take up the call. One soviet soldier wrote home:

> The German mother should curse the day that she bore a son! German women have now to see the horrors of war! They have now to experience what they wanted for other peoples!

What this might mean was revealed in October 1944. Nemmersdorf in East Prussia was the first German village to be occupied by the Red Army, who then temporarily moved out. Exactly what the German military police found when they returned to Nemmersdorf is hard to establish. Göbbels' propaganda machine certainly exaggerated what happened, but maybe not much. The Nazi newspaper headlines were:

- Bolshevik bloodlust rages in east prussian border area
- Bestial murderous terror in east prussia

The article then went on to describe 72 bodies lying in the street, naked women nailed to barn doors, and mass rape of women. Göbbels used the events at Nemmersdorf in a deliberate effort to stiffen German resistance, to persuade Germans to fight on and not surrender.

This probably worked with some, but there was quite a backlash, revealing that the years of unquestioning obedience to the Nazi regime were coming to an end.

1 The local Nazi leader came in for criticism: Why hadn't the civilian population been evacuated? He had not wanted to do this, because it would look like an admission of defeat and, as we have seen, committed Nazis were determined to fight on. However, most of the population of East Prussia now took to the roads, walking or pushing carts with their belongings. They found themselves walking through a war zone, forced to change routes, suffering and dying as winter set in.
2 Elsewhere in Germany people sought to surrender to the Americans or the British, hoping for better treatment (and receiving it).
3 Many were fed up with Göbbels' propaganda and said this kind of treatment was just to be expected:

> ... every thinking person, seeing these gory victims, will immediately contemplate the atrocities which we have perpetrated on enemy soil, and even in Germany. Have we not slaughtered Jews in their thousands? ... By acting in this way we have shown the enemy what they might do to us in the event of their victory. We can't accuse the Russians of behaving just as gruesomely towards other peoples as our own people have done against our own Germans ... After all, what does human life amount to here in Germany?

The Red Army showed no mercy as they advanced across Germany. Homes were looted, civilians robbed: watches were a favourite – some soviet soldiers wore several, all the way up their arms. Many German men were simply shot, especially anyone in uniform, even if he was only a postman or a railway guard. Probably 100,000 were killed by the time the war ended.

Women suffered a different fate as rape became the Red Army's weapon of conquest. Any girl or woman, of any age, was taken, sometimes suffering multiple rapes. Often it was done in front of husbands, sons, fathers to add to the humiliation. Historians estimate that 1.4 million German women were raped in eastern Germany, 100,000 in Berlin alone. For some women, the psychological effects of what was done to them lasted for the rest of their lives. Some managed to blank out the experience: 'I must repress a lot in order, to some extent to be able to live' one woman admitted. Even in these appalling circumstances, Berlin's wry humour crept in. Women noted that the Russians preferred fatter women, and so targeted the wives and mistresses of Nazi officials.

Either before this might happen, through fear, or afterwards, through shame, hundreds of people committed suicide. A cleric in East Prussia recorded: 'Whole good church-going families took their lives, drowned themselves, hanged themselves, slit their wrists, or allowed themselves to be burned along with their homes.' Whole families simply jumped together into the river. Nearly 4000 suicides were recorded in Berlin in the month of April 1945.

The last months of the war were truly terrible for the people of Germany. Along with the hardship caused by lack of food and housing described on previous pages, thousands of refugees began to arrive by train from the east. Some had been travelling for days in open trucks with no food or water. Many had died on the way. They had terrible stories to tell.

It was the ruin of all the Nazis had claimed to exist for.

■ Now make your notes on how the Russians played their part in keeping Germany from surrendering. Use the three headings Faith, Fear and Other Factors.

◁ Civilians escaping to the American zone by crossing the half-destroyed Elbe bridge, April 1945.

■ Concluding your Enquiry

The decision of the Nazi leadership not to surrender before 8 May 1945 was 'without precedent'. In this chapter you have inferred several reasons why the German people kept on fighting for so much longer than might have been expected.

Consider all the notes you have made throughout this enquiry.

Overall, what do you think was the most powerful factor? Was it Faith or Fear or one of the other factors you may have identified? Use the most relevant evidence you have discovered from the five sections to support your decision.

Index